HOW I MET
MY OTHER

TRUE STORIES, TRUE LOVE

Edited by Arielle Haughee

ORANGE BLOSSOM
PUBLISHING

Published 2019 by Orange Blossom Publishing
Maitland, Florida
info@orangeblossombooks.com
www.orangeblossombooks.com

Cover Design: Red Raven Book Design
Interior Formatting: Battle Goddess Productions

Print Edition ISBN: 978-1-949935-00-4
Digital Edition ISBN: 978-1-949935-01-1
Hardcover Edition ISBN: 978-1-949935-02-8
LCCN: 2018965386

All stories are based off true events. Some names and locations have been changed for privacy purposes.

Dedication

To Jean Baker,

Thank you for being my biggest cheerleader and for giving that pesky guy a chance years ago.

-Elle

Acknowledgements

I, first and foremost, would like to thank my husband, Tim, who gave us a second chance after that lousy first date. Thank you for making my life possible and encouraging me every step of the way. The happiness you have given me was the seed for this book. Thank you for all your volunteer hours with all things legal in relation to this project and for listening to me as I talked through every big decision. I was blown away when I asked if you wanted to co-write a story, something you'd never done before, and you said yes. You are generous, loving, hilarious, and all things beautiful in the world.

I would also like to thank my grandmother, Jean Baker, who told me her story and let me share it. You've had an amazing, inspiring life and I am thrilled to give people a window into the wonderful person you are. And also, to my mother who answered dozens, maybe even hundreds, of questions relating to the story, thank you. Your help and support mean more to me than I could ever express.

To all the talented authors who share their stories here, thank you for giving me the gift of your words and for the time you spent crafting them. This book would not have happened without your hard work.

A big thank you to Racquel Henry, my editor, and more

importantly, my friend. You are always there to listen and help whenever I need you and I am so lucky to have you in my life. Thank you for assisting me with this project and all the others I've sent your way. Your expertise and encouragement have been crucial to my journey.

To Fern Goodman, I appreciate your enthusiasm, patience, and understanding. Thank you for your part in this project. And to Dawn Bell, thank you for taking the time to give me the big picture and encouraging me to go for it. You gave me the push I needed to get started.

Last, to Valerie Willis, thank you for the hours and hours you spent guiding me through this process and being my personal guru. I am not sure how I would have done this without you. You are a generous and knowledgeable friend and I appreciate everything you've done for me.

Table of Contents

Be sure to visit www.orangeblossombooks.com to get updates on the couples and see pictures!

Introduction

Love is a mischievous, clever little sprite.

It can sneak up on us when we least expect it, when we are too busy for any of its nonsense. It can hide in the strangest places, oftentimes right in front of our very eyes. It can jump out and tackle us, taking over our entire world.

It also likes to play little jokes, pushing us towards someone we already said *no way* to, insisting we get together. It makes us figure out how to make the impossible work far, far away. It forces us to try over and over and over again when it would be much easier to walk away.

But she gives us a honeyed ambrosia, a bottomless happiness and sense that everything has fallen into place in the world. We are where we belong.

To the lovers, I hope you find reflections of your own story in the words of this book.

To those searching for love, I hope the wide array of how things came to be encourage you to never give up. The sprite never rests.

Arielle

How Sweet It Was

A Rose, Frozen in Time

The Story of Michelle and Brandon
Year: 2001
By Michelle Tweed

Shoulder to shoulder and knee to knee with my fellow passengers, I try again to find a comfortable position. I stagger my feet with the woman across from me to stretch a bit. Easier said than done with me in my Pac Boots and her in her bunny boots. At least my red parka adds some cushion to the netted cargo seat. Our group of about one hundred makes do the best we can to pass the time on the five-hour flight to Antarctica. Some read, some listen to music, some sleep.

Most all of us will have different jobs once we arrive—everything a little town of one thousand will need. We'll have plumbers and welders, recreation staff and hairdressers. Our jobs exist to support the scientists who will also be on station.

"We almost always end up on the same flight, don't we?" the owner of the bunny boots says to me, leaning forward to take a sip from her water bottle.

Her name is Sarah, and she has made this trip many more

times than I have. Her long, silver-blonde hair flows over her blue, fleece jacket as she leans back into her seat.

"Yes! This is my seventh trip down, and I think you've been on at least four of my flights."

I smile back at her then reach under the seat for my water bottle. I also pull out the brand-new journal I've brought along. This will be my longest contract ever. Instead of my normal five months, I will be staying a full year, and I want to write about it. Taking a sip of water, I settle back into my seat. I try to find the words to describe how I feel as I stare down at the blank page.

October 2, 2001

I'm filled with so many emotions today. Just three weeks ago I watched the attacks on the World Trade Center from a TV in the waiting room of the Emergency Department. It was my last day of work there, and I couldn't believe what I was seeing. Fear, uncertainty, and sadness have filled these last few weeks, and I wondered how it might affect my trip. Could I leave my family and friends behind? Would one of my flights end in the same fate?

Now, here I sit on the last of six flights after leaving my home in Minnesota a week ago. I'm hopeful for the year ahead. Sad for saying goodbye to family and friends back home. Excited to see friends who will be returning to the ice. And a little nervous for the year ahead. I wonder how much of a toll the winter months will take on me mentally.

Even with all of this weighing on me, I have a feeling deep within that I've never had before. I don't know what to call it. An awakening, an awareness, a realization.... I'm not sure. But I

6

have a new joy. I feel God is working in me and I hope and pray that I will be brave enough to listen to His plan and follow it. Maybe it's something very simple, I don't know, but whatever it is, it is strong and deep within me.

I'm going to take this year to work on me. And even though I've been single for a while, I don't plan on dating anyone. This is a year of growth. No distractions. Besides, I don't have to worry about passing up "Mr. Right." I've said for years the man I'm going to marry will give me my first red rose. My friends and I have joked about this for so long, that I've actually started to believe it, and hope it will come true. And since there are no roses in Antarctica, I won't have to worry about that.

Laughing a little to myself, I continue to write and stay lost in my thoughts, wondering what this year of growth will bring, and what this new feeling means. I can't help but feel my life will soon be changing direction.

The plane hits turbulence, and I am jolted back to reality. An Air National Guard crewman announces over the loudspeaker that we have begun our descent and to prepare for landing. Everyone around me begins to put their cold weather gear back on.

There are no windows near me, so I have no idea how low or how close we are. It's a guessing game as to when we will touch down. After roughly half an hour of anticipation, the wheels hit the ice and the powerful rush of the airplane throws us all a little sideways in our seats. The plane comes to a stop, and the door is opened. A blast of cold, dry air rushes through and burns my nostrils. Blinding light floods in from the nearby door, and we all stand and start to shuffle in that direction. Squinting, I grab my sunglasses from the top pocket of my parka. All I can see is white snow and blue ice.

Walking down the stairs, leading from the plane to the sea ice, I pass a man wearing brown bibs, a brown jacket, and a knit purple hat. He points to a line of passenger vehicles and yells over the engine noise to keep moving and not to stop for pictures.

I hear him repeat this several times until his voice drowns out in the distance. A thin layer of snow squeaks like Styrofoam under my boots, while a slight breeze stings my face and fills my nose with the scent of diesel exhaust.

In the near distance, just beyond the row of busses, there's a line of about fifteen little square huts on skis. A few red trucks and yellow forklifts are dotted in-between.

I make my way toward the large red bus waiting first in line. Its wheels are as tall as me, and the words on the side read, "Ivan the Terra Bus."

I climb the stairs into the large bus, and the driver greets me.

"Michelle, you're back," she says, smiling wide.

"Hi, Gloria!" I stop to give her a quick hug.

Her tiny frame, dressed in jeans and a fleece jacket, looks even smaller sitting behind the giant steering wheel.

"Yep, I'm back, and for a full year this time," I tell her. "I'm a glutton for punishment!"

"Well, I'd say," she says, smiling.

Laughing, I sling my orange bag behind me then squeeze my way down the aisle and into a seat. I take the first empty spot and slide over to the window. Soon the bus is full, and we start the slow journey across the ice toward town. These busses are definitely not built for speed.

The view from my window is of a vast mountain range. It stretches out across the flat expanse of ice, and it is breathtaking. White snow covers the black peaks, with bowl-shaped valleys in between. It reminds me of an enormous ice cream sundae, with marshmallow cream flowing over the edges and through the cracks of the chocolaty mountains. I have been coming here since I was nineteen, and this place still amazes me with its beauty.

Our destination sits opposite the mountains, on a little island formed by the still active volcano, Mt Erebus. From here, the completely snow-covered volcano looms like a giant over the town with its white plume rising and marching across the clear blue sky.

As we approach, I notice a new sign has been put up. It reads, "The National Science Foundation welcomes you to McMurdo Station, Antarctica."

I sigh to myself, "Home sweet home."

The bus makes its way up the hill to the center of town. We pull up to a large tan building. Building 155 houses the dining hall, several offices, and some dorm rooms. Gloria opens the door, and we all begin to squeeze back down the aisle.

Going up the stairs and into 155, I am greeted by several old friends. It's like a large family reunion as we all hug and laugh and tell stories of what we have been up to. Our reunion is cut short as those who have just arrived are herded into the dining hall for orientation and dorm keys.

The next few days are filled with long hours of training new dispatchers. Our office is a tiny room inside the firehouse, with our only window looking out into the bay of firetrucks. There are four dispatchers, including myself as the lead. Our job is to monitor vehicle and foot traffic in and out of town, the 911 line, and a fire alarm panel. We are also the town operator and trouble desk.

October 5, 2001

Well, I'm here and settled in. It's been fun seeing all my old friends. We've been meeting up at the bar or in a lounge every night since I got here. This place seriously feels more like home to me than being back in Minnesota. I love it here.

My second week starts just as my first. On Tuesday, I make my way to the dining hall for dinner. Tired from too many days working past my normal 12-hour shift, I stand with my tray of food and scan the room for a place to sit. Soon, I hear someone call out my name.

"Michelle, come join us," Jill says, waving.

Jill is one of the new dispatchers and is sitting at a round table with three men. I smile and walk over to them. She introduces me to everyone, and I take a seat. It's the first year down for all of them, so dinner is spent mostly answering questions about town, the nearby New Zealand base, and the surrounding hiking trails. We finish up and go our separate ways for the evening.

The next day I train Jill in the dispatch office.

"So, Michelle, are you seeing anyone?" Jill quizzes with a sly smile.

Laughing, I reply, "Well, I am single, but I don't plan on dating anyone this year."

"Okay, but I know a guy that's interested if you change your mind. He's really nice," she adds.

She doesn't say who it is, but I'm pretty sure I know who she's talking about. At the table the night before, the only man she knew herself was sitting to her left. I can't recall his name, but they had sat together on the long flight from Los Angeles to Auckland and had gotten to know each other a bit.

"All right," I shrug. I wonder to myself if this will make things awkward now when he's around. I don't want to date anyone this year. Besides, I didn't really think he was that good looking.

A couple days later I'm at Southern Exposure, one of the bars in town, saying goodbye to a couple of friends who are scheduled to leave the next day. On my way back to our table, with a round of drinks, I notice Jill's friend sitting at a corner table with two other men.

Stopping by, I smile and say, "Hello, you're Jill's friend, aren't you?"

"Yeah, hi," he says, taking off his hat.

I adjust my tray of drinks and ask with uncertainty, "Is it Brad?"

"Brandon," He answers, not seeming to care that I didn't remember his name.

"Oh, I'm sorry. I'm horrible at remembering names." I apologize with a grin. "Have you gotten settled in yet?"

"Yeah. I'm liking it down here. It's not too different from where I grew up in North Dakota." He takes a sip of his beer and smiles.

"Are you here for the summer, or did you sign up for a full year?" I ask.

"Just the summer, I'm scheduled to leave in February. How about you?"

"I signed up for a full year. I've never done a winter before, so it'll be interesting." I glance over at my friends to make sure they aren't missing me or their drinks yet. "Hopefully, I won't be too toasty by the end. I'm not sure how I'll handle the four and a half months of complete darkness. Not to mention the town dropping down to around two hundred, with no flights in or out for six months. But I guess there's only one way to find out," I say, and smile.

We continue to make small talk about work and town, and I notice things about him I hadn't before. He has the friendliest eyes, with dark eyebrows to frame them. His dark, almost black short hair goes well against his tanned face. As we talk and laugh together, I realize just how handsome he is. Now, feeling suddenly shy, my mind goes blank. I search for a way to end the conversation before he notices.

"Well, I'd better get these drinks over to my friends. They're starting to look pretty thirsty." I laugh nervously, feeling flushed. "See you around."

We don't speak the rest of the evening, but now and then I find myself glancing his way.

By the third week, town seems to have found its flow of work and play. With a diverse group of people from all over the United States, there are several opportunities for free classes and different events. Sign-up sheets outside the Rec office have everything from sign language to belly dancing.

I sign up for swing dance lessons, bartending, to be a DJ at the little radio station, and to drive the big balloon-tired delta vehicles to lead tours to the ice caves. I run into Brandon from time to time, and every time I do I find myself liking him more and more.

The next Tuesday, I'm scheduled to drive a group to the ice caves, so I stop by the Rec office to see who has signed up and notice Brandon's name. My heart skips a beat. I'm both nervous and excited. Jill's name is on the sheet as well.

That evening, those who signed up gather in front of the dining hall, as I pull up in the orange delta vehicle. There is room for two passengers up front with me, and the rest will sit in the rear cab. A bonus to having twenty-four-hours of daylight is that you can do anything outside, at any time of the day, and it's still bright out.

"Jill!" I wave, seeing her in the crowd after stepping around the back to open the door to the passenger cab. "Why don't you sit up front with me? I have room for one more if you want to ask someone." I hope she will pick Brandon.

She does, and they climb up in the front cab. We make our way out of town and start the slow drive across the sea ice to the ice caves. This time I am happy for the long forty-five-minute drive.

"So, Brandon, how did you find out about working in Antarctica?" I ask, already knowing Jill's answer and hoping to learn more about Brandon.

"I was working as an electrician in Denver. A co-worker told me there was going to be a job fair that weekend, and they were looking for electricians to work at the South Pole. I thought he was crazy at first, but I wanted to get out of Denver. There's just too many people there." He removes his parka. The cab warms up with the sun beaming in and glaring off the ice. "So, I decided to go, fully expecting not to get hired. But they called, and here I am. How did you hear about this place, Michelle?"

I take a deep breath and adjust my sunglasses. "Oh, I sort of grew up with it. My dad started coming down when I was five, and then my uncle. When I turned nineteen, I didn't like college and didn't know what direction I wanted to go in. So, I decided to come down for one summer only, and then head back to college. Well, that was seven seasons ago," I say, laughing. "I just love it here. I knew after my very first week of my first season I would come back again. But I didn't think I'd be coming back for this many years. It gets in your blood. The people are amazing, it's beautiful, and the opportunities to travel once we leave are wonderful."

"I see what you're saying," Brandon replies. "I'm loving this place. I was actually hired to work at the Pole as an electrician, but when I got to New Zealand, they told me I was going to be at McMurdo. Someone didn't pass the physical, so they needed me here." He clears his throat and takes a sip from his water bottle. "But I'm not too sad about the change in assignment," he says.

The three of us talk and laugh the entire way. Once we arrive, I stop the delta and we all pile out. As we walk up to the glacier wall, the entrance to the ice caves is a mere crack. But as we step inside, a gorgeous cavern of blue and white ice unfolds. In some spots, hexagon-shaped crystals, two to three inches in diameter, line the walls and ceiling. Many are layered in clusters, one on top of another, and jut out several inches. They are so clear and thick that they almost look fake, like they could be made of plastic. Other parts in the cave are smooth, with frozen waterfalls and ice that seems to have been sculpted by the hand of an artist.

We slide and climb around, inside and out, for a good two hours before heading back to town. Jill and Brandon sit up front again, and we laugh and talk some more. When we reach McMurdo, I drop them and the other passengers off at the dining hall, a little sad for the night to be over.

October 23, 2001

Well, it's been a while since I wrote, but I thought tonight was a good night to start again. I've met someone. I know, I said I wasn't going to date anyone this year. But he's very handsome. And so nice. His name's Brandon. We just went to the ice caves together. Well, not together, but he was there, and we hung out quite a bit. It was so fun! I'm starting to like him. But he's only here for the summer, so I think I'll just keep it as friends. It's not worth getting into something just to have him leave. I'm here this year to focus on myself and my own journey.

October 25, 2001

Brandon called me at work last night just to thank me for driving him to the ice caves. He even said Jill told him not to call—too desperate—but he wanted to call anyway. I was so excited and nervous I could barely find anything to say. Then, tonight, I was sure I wouldn't hear from him. But while I was in dispatch training one of the firefighters, he stopped by to say

HOW I MET MY OTHER

hello. I think I'm doomed with this one!

The upcoming Saturday is the town Halloween party. It's always the biggest party of the year, with almost everyone dressing up. I make my way down to the party with a couple of friends. Walking inside the gym, we throw our parkas onto an ever-growing pile of other parkas near the door. We head into the crowd, walking under the parachutes hanging from the ceiling.

Along the way, we stop to visit with friends and admire the different costumes. For being in Antarctica, the costumes are incredibly creative. There are the usual goblins and ghosts, and other pre-made costumes people bring down in their luggage. But others go all out, making something out of scrap materials they find around town.

As we walk through the crowd, we see a man paddling a canoe, a helicopter, and a Chinese dragon. It's not long before I run into Brandon. He's wearing a silver helmet, and what looks to be armor and a shield.

"Nice costume," I yell over the music. "Are you supposed to be a knight?"

"You got it!" he yells back. "I found the helmet in the Rec office, and I made the rest out of cardboard and duct tape."

"It's great!" I adjust my long black wig and witch's hat, as we are bumped around by the crowd.

"Do you want to dance?" he asks, pointing toward the dance floor.

"Sure." I take his hand as he leads the way.

We dance and talk, song after song. When the DJ finally plays a slow song, we stay on the dance floor. He pulls me close, but not too close, and we begin to sway to the music.

Leaning over, he says, "I would ask you out to dinner and a movie, but it's kind of hard here."

"Well, there's always the burger bar at Gallagher's," I say with a smile. My heart flutters in my chest.

"Yeah, I guess that could work," he replies.

When the party's over, we all head up to the dining hall to see if any food has been left out. Brandon and I sit at a table with some friends and talk into the wee hours of the morning. At around three o'clock most everyone is gone, and Brandon, too tired to stay longer, dismisses himself. I stay and talk with the last few friends remaining. We are currently on night shift and like to keep those hours even on nights off.

The next evening I'm working in dispatch when Brandon stops in.

"Sorry for not walking you home last night," he says.

"Oh, that's okay, I'm a big girl." I smile and shuffle through some papers on my desk.

"So, can I take you out for a burger at Gallagher's this Friday?" he asks, absentmindedly playing with the zipper pull on his jacket.

"Sure, I'd love that!"

Every Friday, burgers are made fresh to order at the non-smoking bar. There are no restaurants in town, so this is the closest thing he can do to buying me dinner.

"Okay, I'll pick you up at your place. Say eight o'clock? We might have to walk. My car's in the shop," he jokes.

HOW I MET MY OTHER

No one has access to a vehicle other than for work purposes. Laughing, I accept, and we talk a while more before he heads home.

November 1, 2001

Okay, so I sort of broke my rule for this season. Tomorrow I'm going on a date with Brandon. I'm so excited, but I'm so scared. He seems like such a great guy, and I couldn't turn him down. But, I'm afraid to get attached, just to have him leave in February, and me to be stuck here until September. And what if the only reason he asked me out was because he heard the old saying that if you don't have a girlfriend by Halloween, you'll be alone for the season? No, I can't think like that. He has been stopping by work or calling me almost every day since the ice caves. I'm just going to go out with him tomorrow and be 100% myself.

Friday arrives, and he meets me at my room ten minutes early. I grab my parka, and we walk the short distance across town to Gallagher's. He gets the burgers while I get the drinks, and we meet over at a little round corner table for two.

"Well, this will be interesting, dating at the bottom of the world. We can't even go watch a sunset together until February," he says, as he laughs and takes a sip of his beer.

"Yeah, we'll just have to be creative." I play with the little pink straw in my mixed drink.

We talk and laugh the entire evening until bar close. He walks me to my room, and after opening my door, I turn toward him. He reaches out, hugs me, and says goodnight.

A Rose, Frozen in Time

November 2, 2001

We just had our date, and it went GREAT! We talked the entire evening. We have so much in common. It just went so well. He was such a gentleman when he walked me to my room tonight. He didn't even try to go for a kiss. I hate kissing on the first date. It's just so weird.

The next night is Saturday, and there's a disco party planned at Gallagher's. I'm scheduled to work, but Jill catches me in the hall and says she'll switch with me.

Excited, I decide not to tell Brandon, hoping to surprise him. But, as I'm in my room getting ready, he calls.

"Hey! Jill told me you switched schedules for tonight. Do you want me to come over and we can go to the party together?" he asks, clearing his throat like he wants to say something else, but then doesn't.

"Sure, come on over. You've got to see everyone in my dorm. They look hilarious," I say and pull on my knee-high black boots. I am slightly disappointed that I don't get to surprise him, but so happy he called right after hearing I had the night off.

He comes right over. My door's open and he walks in.

"Nice outfit. I love the pigtails," he says, swishing his hand through my hair. "I hope you don't mind. I didn't get dressed up this time."

"No, I don't mind. I'm not dressed in disco either. I brought this little flower dress down with me. I figured it would work well at some party. I'm thinking, flower power," I say, making the peace sign with my hands.

He laughs, "Well, you look great."

We head down to the pre-party in the lounge. Everyone there looks straight out of the 70's, complete with afros and bell bottoms.

Tugging at my short dress, I pull on my parka, and we go to leave for the bar. "Can you believe the parties that go on down here?" I ask.

"I know! No one is going to believe me back home if I tell them what life is really like here. They all think I'm freezing my butt off in some igloo," he says, laughing as he holds the door.

We arrive at the bar. Steam pours out from the open door as we walk through the group of smokers standing just outside. Squeezing through the crowd, we head in and dance the night away.

The last song of the evening is always a slow one. This time he holds me very close. Before I can register what song is playing, he tells me he has asked his boss if he can extend his contract and stay the full year.

My heart leaps in my chest. *Is this really happening?* Then I hear the song we are dancing to. It's Etta James, *At Last*. I can't help but wonder if it might be true. *Has my love really come along?*

I'm not sure of it, and we are so close, but I swear he just lightly kissed my shoulder. The air is hot, and the crowd is thick, but to me, we are the only two here.

The bar closes, and we make our way outside. Squinting, we both grab for our sunglasses. The sun is shining bright tonight. We stop for a short time at an after party in one of the lounges, and then he walks me home.

I open my door and turn shyly back to him, unsure of what he is expecting. But he just leans in and gives me a little kiss and a hug.

Then, just as he is letting go, he says, "Let me try that again."

He moves in for another kiss, and I totally freeze. I give him a little kiss and a hug again and say goodnight.

As I close the door, I want to die. I feel so stupid, but I'm just not ready for anything more than a peck. I want to take things slow.

Over the next four days, we spend quite a bit of time together in my room watching movies and talking for hours. And when I'm working, he still calls to say hi.

On Wednesday evening, I'm at work when he stops in.

"Hi." My eyes gleam. "What brings you by?" I try to mask my excitement by finishing up a note in the vehicle travel log.

"Well, I went and looked all over town for some flowers for you today, but this is all I could find." He pulls his hand out of his jacket pocket, and with it, a metal rose.

He holds it out in the palm of his hand. It's about six inches long with red petals and a dark oil slick-colored stem with leaves.

"A guy in my shop makes these. The petals are red from the way he heat treats them." He places it gently into my waiting hands.

The cool metal touches my fingers, and my heart melts. He brought me a red rose. In a land where there are none, he found one and brought it to me. Is my dream of marrying the man who gives me my first red rose about to die...or has life just been breathed into it?

"It's beautiful," I say, coming back to the moment. "I love it!" I step around the desk, pulling him into my arms, and we kiss. This time my lips linger just a bit longer.

Get an update on Michelle and Brandon and see pictures at www.orangeblossombooks.com

Love in Marabella

The Story of Michael and Deborah
Year: 1978
By Racquel Henry

When you notice her it will be in the crowded Kingdom Hall. She will be wearing a white dress with sleeves that lace together and tie in a knot at the shoulder bone. It is the kind of dress a girl like her would get married in. There will be a group of guys crowded around her and her two sisters. They are the stars of the congregation. They are the Revanales sisters—everyone in Trinidad wants to attend their parties. It isn't an event without them.

You walk up to the circle of friends, casual, keeping it cool. You're on the opposite side of where she's standing but you can't stop staring at her. You've never laid eyes on a girl like that and you take in her golden brown afro, her light brown eyes. Her eyes catch yours for a split second and your heart ping-pongs in your chest. Beat up. Beat down. Beat up. Beat down. It picks up speed and you want to deny what it is, but it's too late—you already know. And then you have to know her name, so you inch your way to the other side.

"Hello," you say.

She smiles. You swear the world froze for a second and then you say, "I'm Michael."

"Deborah," she says. She smiles again and your heart isn't beating on its normal schedule anymore. Then one of her sisters leans over to whisper something in her ear and the moment is lost.

You devise a plan. You are not allowed to be alone with her. She isn't allowed to date and neither are you, really. Her mother is a devout Witness and she'd be damned if she was going to let any of her young daughters go on dates with boys she didn't know—boys whose intentions she isn't familiar with. You are known around Marabella as DJ KC. You are the most sought after DJ and so you make a move to invite Deborah to a house party your friends are throwing. You even offer to pick up her and her sisters because they have no car and they don't drive. You go out of your way to make sure everything is perfect. You have your playlist all set up. You will impress her with your music selection and when one of the slow songs come on, you will ask her to dance.

You spend the whole day getting ready. You make sure your side burns are perfectly shaped and you will wear your best disco outfit, which is really just black high-waisted bell bottom pants, a white shirt, and platform shoes. You load all your DJ equipment into the car and you even arrive five minutes early. If they aren't quite ready, you'd be cool with waiting. You open the gate at the front, make your way to the gallery, and call out, "Ms. Baptiste, it's Michael!" The gallery is locked but the door is open. There's a warm glow from the light on inside and it smells like curry. It makes your mouth water and you sigh because in all your preparation, you had forgotten to eat dinner.

Ms. Baptiste comes out of the door and steps into the gallery. She's got her hair slicked down like she's just come out of the shower and she's wearing a pink floral duster.

"Hello," you say, the nerves shooting through you. But you can tell that something isn't right. There's a vibe on that gallery and even though you can't quite put your finger on it, it makes your stomach feel like a well.

"Deborah, Annie, and Lynn won't be going with you tonight," she says, folding her arms across her chest.

You try to process if what you just heard was accurate. "Is everything okay? Is Deborah or the girls sick?" you ask, even though you are the one who feels sick.

"No. They're just not going because I changed my mind," she says, her eyes glassy and challenging in the dark night.

You know better than to cross her so you say, "Okay. I'm sorry to hear that. I guess I'll see them at the meeting then. Have a good night, Sister Baptiste."

You make the walk back to your car, but your feet are heavy and your heart is like acid in your chest. It's not that far of a walk, but you're walking so slow it feels like it's taken you hours. You won't get to see Deborah tonight. It isn't fair. The worst part is you can't control any of it. The rest of the night you can't get yourself together. You scratch records as you DJ, the transitions to all of your songs are off, and you feel like your head is up in space. The stereo system even blows up. You're there at the party, but you're not really there.

You get the idea that maybe Deborah would like to come and work for your company. You need a receptionist and you know she would be the perfect fit. Not only is she smart, but she's easy on the eyes. On top of that, you could talk to her without her mother looking over her shoulder. This would be business and if there's one thing that Ms. Baptiste liked, it's money. Anything the girls made when they worked had to be given to their mom for what she called *household expenses.*

So, one day after a meeting at the Kingdom Hall, you see Deborah at the water fountain near the door. She's wearing a blush colored dress and a flower that matches in her light brown afro. Your heart skips a beat and you muster up the courage to go talk to her. She finishes her sip and smiles when she sees you standing before her.

"Hey, Michael," she says.

You pause for a beat and then mentally snap yourself out of the trance. "Hey, you say. That was a good talk, right?" you ask.

"Yes, Brother Thompson always delivers the best talks," she says.

You swallow. "I was wondering something. I need someone to help out with the administrative stuff in my business. I was wondering if you were looking for work?" There you said it. It's out in the universe now. There was nothing else you could do. If it was meant to be then the universe would make it happen, if it wasn't then that would be that. It really isn't up to you anymore.

"I would love to get a job, but I have to see if Mami will let me first. Can I let you know next meeting?" she asks, her eyes mesmerizing you.

"Sure," you say, hope rising fast within. You add, "No rush on a decision." And it's true because you would wait forever for her if it meant she'd come work for you at some point.

"Great. I'll let you know," she says. She looks past you.

When you turn around you see her sisters waving her over.

"I gotta go. See you later," she says. She smiles that same smile that makes your heart a puddle on the sidewalk.

You open your mouth to say bye, but she's already gone, racing over to meet her sisters. You watch as they giggle at each other and head out of the Kingdom Hall doors.

On her first day you can feel it's the start of something new, something good. When she walks into your building, she reminds you of what you picture magic to be: vibrant, sparkling and as wondrous as the universe. You know right away that if you were going to call anywhere home, it cannot exist without her.

You show her around and tell her what she'll be doing. All the while your heart is a reckless mess of beats in your chest. You think to yourself that it must be doing at minimum a million beats per second. You make up your mind that you're going to ask her to lunch.

You approach her at her new desk. You tried to give her the best spot in the office. As you walk towards her you study her, memorize the lines of her refined jawline and the polished texture of her styled afro. She's looking down at a stack of papers on her desk. You never want to forget how she looks in this moment.

"Hey," you say, and clear your throat when you realize your voice comes out a little strained. "Do you want to go grab lunch?"

She looks up from the stack of papers and smiles. It is the same smile you have been watching for a while, the smile that glimmers and stops time all at once.

"I'll have to check with my boss first. I just have so much work to get through," she says. The smile doesn't leave her face.

"Something tells me he wouldn't mind," you say, your lips curling into a smirk.

"All right, then," she says standing up from the desk, "just let me grab my purse." She opens the metal drawer beneath her desk and takes out the black purse, then swings it over her shoulder.

As the two of you make your way out of the building, you say, "How about a doubles and a red solo?"

Deborah nods.

Your plan works. While Deborah works for you, the two of you get so close that you become inseparable. You go to lunches every day now and before long it becomes understood that neither of you want to go out with anyone else. But Deborah isn't allowed to call you her boyfriend, and you're not allowed to call her your girlfriend. So you don't put any labels on it. You are completely enraptured. From the moment you saw her that day in the Kingdom Hall, you have been in a trance—the kind of trance that everyone hopes to be in, but not everyone gets to. It is the kind of trance one never wants to get out of. Your friends call you sensitive, but you don't care. You are a man in love. A man who knows exactly who he wants to spend the rest of his life with.

You start thinking of ways you'll propose. You can't stand not having a label another second. You want the labels. You want to tell the world that she's the love of your life. You want her to be your wife, she's already your whole world.

But first, you have to get permission from Sister Baptiste. Just thinking about asking her makes your soul rumble. You are restless and can't sleep for weeks. Then you think, *Grow up, Mike. You're a grown man.* Plus, she can be tough, but she's always liked you well enough. She trusted you to drive her daughters around.

You finally muster up the nerve. You get yourself together, buy the ring, make sure your ducks are in a row. You shave and clean up well before you make the drive over to Sister Baptiste's house, where you hope your future wife lives.

You get out of the car and make your way to the gallery.

"Hi, Sister Baptiste! It's Mike!" you call from the other side. You remember that time you came by and she didn't let the girls go to the party. You shake the image away. Now is not the time to remember negative memories.

Instead, you see Deborah come out the front door. Her glow is so bright and warm you'd think she had the light of a million suns inside her.

"Hey, Mike," she says, her eyes dazzling.

"Hey," you say.

She unlocks the lock on the gallery entrance and gives you a hug. You savor the moment, let yourself absorb some of that warmth you noticed earlier. You need as much positive energy as possible for what you're about to do.

Sister Baptiste is seated at the dining table cleaning seim. She glances at you over her glasses. "Oh, hey, Michael," she says, still tending to the bowl of beans in front of her.

You take a deep breath. "Hey, Sister Baptiste. I hope these girls aren't making you do too much work around here," you say, shifting and noticing that everything in your body suddenly feels uncomfortable.

She gives a little laugh, but she's pretty focused on her task at hand.

"So, Sister," you say, trying to steady your voice and not run screaming in the other direction. "Would you mind if I sat down to speak with you?"

"Come, sit," she says, motioning to an empty chair in front of her. She keeps her head down, concentrating on the bowl. She only briefly glances up to look at the chair and uses the knife to point to it.

Deborah looks at you and her brows wrinkle in confusion.

You smile at her, but it's really more of a half-smile. You can feel it. You make your way over to the table and Deborah follows you. When you sit down, she sits next to you. Once you sit, you think about what to do with your hands so you decide to clasp them together and stretch your arms out on the table.

You clear your throat, "Sister Baptiste, I have a very serious question to ask you."

She stops cleaning the seim and looks up, for real this time.

She's peering at you over her glasses. Her eyes are serious and focused on you. Does she know what you're about to ask?

"I've known your daughter for a while now and I've come to the realization that she's the only one I want to spend time with...forever," you say.

She drops the knife in the bowl and adjusts her glasses so that they are no longer on the edge of her nose. You try not to let her appearance, her attention on you, intimidate you.

"What I'm trying to say is that I love your daughter very much and I'd like to ask your permission to marry her."

For a moment there is dead silence and then a cackle pierces the air. She's laughing at you. She thinks it's funny that you want to spend the rest of your life with Deborah.

You glance at Deborah. She frowns and places a hand on your arm. She shifts her attention back to her mother, her frown remaining intact. "What's so funny, Mami?"

Sister Baptiste slaps her knee and stops laughing for a minute. She wipes a tear from her eye. "Look at her," she says, pointing to Deborah. "Look at my daughter. You think you can take care of her?" she asks.

She might as well have thrown brick to your head. You connect the dots and realize she doesn't think you're good enough.

"Yes, I do think I can take care of her," you say. You know you can, but you are almost certain that your voice is unconvincing. The sounds in the room suddenly feel so loud, it's like you have to fight to be heard, to be taken seriously.

"You're not even the right skin tone—you're too dark for her."

HOW I MET MY OTHER

This time the brick to your head has cracked your skull.

"Mami, why are you acting like this?" Deborah asks.

Sister Baptiste is up from her seat now. She is a short woman at five feet or so, but right now she feels like a giant, the way she makes her seriousness known. "Leave. You need to get out of my house."

"I love your daughter, Sister Baptiste. Haven't you always entrusted me with her care?"

"Leave," Sister Baptiste says.

You don't know what else to do. You glance at Deborah and her mouth just hangs open.

"And you," Sister Baptiste says, pointing to Deborah, "you go inside. Go to your room."

You see Marge, Deborah's oldest sister, appear from the hallway. You didn't even realize she was home. She grabs Deborah by the arm, dragging her into the nearest bedroom. You never imagined that asking permission to marry Deborah would have resulted in a scene like this. You feel yourself split open and you are exposed. You are a mockery. You hang your head and stare at your shoes.

"Marge," Sister Baptiste says, "Get a pot of water boiling. If he won't leave then we'll have to force him out."

Your eyes widen when you process what she's threatening to do with that water, so you hustle out the front door. Once you're on the other side of that gate, you gulp the air because you're out of breath. You're not exactly sure why—it's not that far of a pathway. But it's like you just ran a marathon and your muscles are sore, your lungs desperate for air and your heart exhausted.

You look around and everything seems like it's from a foreign country. You want a sign, someone, anyone, to tell you what to do next. And then the thought comes to you: Deborah's brother, Glen. He'll know what to do.

It's been a month since Glen stormed into Sister Baptiste's house and demanded that Deborah come stay with him. Since then, you've been able to see and talk to Deborah whenever you wanted. And even though you wish like hell her mother liked you, the whole fiasco at the house changed nothing for you. It never would.

So you ask Deborah to a movie one night at your favorite theater: Empire. The two of you had been there a few times with some other friends from the congregation. You slip the ring you bought a month ago in your pocket. You had hoped to propose in front of Deborah's friends and family, but obviously that isn't going to work out—and you aren't going to wait a second longer. In front of your favorite movie theater is the next best choice.

The whole movie you fidget and try to get your nerves under control. Deborah keeps stealing glances at you.

"Why are you acting so strange?" she whispers in the middle of the movie.

"Strange?" you whisper back. Leave it to her to call you out.

She raises an eyebrow.

God she's beautiful. You slip your hand into hers. "I love you," you whisper.

"Love you too," she says. She rests her head on your shoulder.

HOW I MET MY OTHER

After the movie, while everyone shuffles out of the theater, you get down on one knee. This is it. When people see what you're doing, they stop to marvel.

Deborah's eyes get glassy and she covers her mouth with one hand.

"Deborah, from the moment I saw you, I knew I wanted to spend the rest of my life with you. Your energy has totally enraptured me. With you I feel like I can take on the world. Will you marry me, my baby?"

"Yes, Mike, of course I will," she says.

You slide the ring on her finger and stand up. You wrap your arms around her and press your lips to hers. If you never have another big moment in life besides this one, you'll be all right. Your queen has said yes.

Get an update on Michael and Deborah and see pictures at www.orangeblossombooks.com

A Heart Guarded

The Story of Chelsea and Brandon
Year: 2002
By Chelsea Fuchs

Guard your heart above all else, for it determines the course of your life.

Proverbs 4:23 NLT

They *should* stay friends. That's as far as she'd let her heart think. Friends were good. Friends were safe. Friends would always be there for one another. And Brandon had been there for her. Even when things had spun out of control.

It started innocently enough.

When exactly they met had always been a point of contention. Brandon swore it was the first day of band camp before their freshmen year. Chelsea remembered seeing the boy in the red flannel coat but hadn't paid any attention to him until after Labor Day Weekend. Whenever they'd met, the one thing they agreed on was the event that solidified their friendship.

HOW I MET MY OTHER

It had been the spring band trip to Dallas their freshman year. They cruised the Galleria and dreamed about what it would be like when they grew up. Chelsea wanted to be rich but not famous. Brandon promised to be her bodyguard. After all, he was already in weightlifting class.

Since it was Texas, it only made sense that there would be a dance floor in the center the steakhouse where they went to dinner. The pair took to the dance floor. They danced like no one was watching as they made up their own Tango moves to the beat of the country band.

Brandon became Chelsea's haven in the storm that was high school. She felt she could be her truest self when she was around him. "I've always wanted a big brother," she commented as they laid in the grass one afternoon and pointed out animals in the clouds.

"I'll be your big brother," he replied as he played with her hand.

"You can't be my big brother, I'm ten days older than you."

"I'm bigger. I can be your big little brother." They pinky promised. Brandon extended his protective services to included Chelsea's little sister, Tiff.

One day a boy who liked Tiff dared to breach the inner circle of friends and have lunch with her. Brandon walked over, grabbed the boy's bottle of soda and tightened the lid so it wouldn't come off. They never saw the boy again.

"Brandon," Chelsea scolded while trying to hold back laughter, "why did you do that?"

"He's not good enough for Tiff."

Chelsea might not have gotten the older brother she'd always wanted, but Tiff sure had.

A friend asked Chelsea why she didn't just date Brandon and get it over with. He was good-looking, she was good-looking, they would be good-looking together.

"If I dated him, I'd have to marry him. And I'm not ready to get married," Chelsea had joked. She wasn't going to waste her precious time on meaningless relationships that just ended in heartbreak. And a relationship with Brandon wouldn't be meaningless. She wasn't ready for that.

"Lighten up, no one is saying you have to get married. Just loosen up and have some fun." The advice from her friend contradicted her values. She couldn't be like that.

It was bad enough that he was so close to her mom and sister. He'd even taken her grandma out for a smoothie.

"Geez, Chelsea," her grandma had said. "I thought Brandon was a dweeb, the way you explained him. But he's gorgeous. What's wrong with you?"

She was elected to several leadership positions. It's what she wanted. She'd been reading leadership books since she was fourteen and loved being able to help those around her. She had responsibilities and couldn't let those counting on her down. Chelsea was going to get her degree in Chemical Engineering and become the CEO of a Fortune 500 company before she was thirty-five. Boys were distractions, and she'd seen how people completely changed their lives for relationships that just resulted in broken hearts. She had to stay focused, study hard, and work even harder. She still hadn't given up the thought of being the first Supreme Court Justice that was also an LPGA Champion.

First, she was going to conquer the corporate world. And she'd have to practice her putting. She didn't have time for a boyfriend, for anything, that would distract her from her goals.

One day senior year Chelsea slammed her locker closed and balanced the stack of textbooks on her leg while she struggled to shove them in her backpack. Her trombone teetered back and forth. She was running late. Again.

Her golf coach was going to be pissed. The debate team meeting had run long, and her history partner was about to walk out the door. If she didn't hurry, Chelsea would have to wait until tomorrow to figure out which chapters she was supposed to cover for the history project.

The rest of her week was packed full. After the daily golf practices, she had a choir concert, a golf tournament, a debate fundraiser, not to mention the planning meeting for the Bible Club Lock-In. If she didn't get her part of the history project done tonight, she wouldn't have time before it was due and they'd all fail. She couldn't let the others down.

It was in that moment Brandon strolled into the band locker room. "Hey, Chelsea."

"Oh, hi." The trombone tipped further to the side. She grabbed it by the handle before it crashed. "I don't have time to talk to you right now, I'm running late."

She ran past him, thinking her simple explanation would be enough. He was usually patient with her crazy schedule and sometimes unreasonable demands. She'd caught up to her partner and asked her question before she ran out the door again.

The next day she saw Brandon and flashed him a smile. "Hi!"

He walked past her and avoided eye contact. Chelsea frowned. That wasn't normal for Brandon.

"What's up with Brandon?" Chelsea asked her close friend, Joe.

"Yesterday he was pretty upset. He said that you were *too busy* to talk to him, so now he's *too busy* to talk to you."

Chelsea wondered if it was that simple. He usually didn't mind if he was on the bottom of her to-do list, as long as she got around to talking to him, eventually. He'd said so. She was sure this would blow over.

So it began, the fight that wasn't a fight. The breakup that wasn't a breakup, of the couple that wasn't a couple.

When Brandon handed Chelsea a note a few days later, she hoped it was for a truce—she missed him. It wasn't.

Dear Chelsea,

The way you have been treating me and acting lately isn't fair. You are rude and inconsiderate. You shouldn't treat people this way.

I'm just telling you this so you can change.

Love your "big brother,"

Brandon

After school that day, Chelsea spied Brandon in the surprisingly empty band locker room. Armed with the "explanation" letter from him, she decided it was time to talk. She needed to stay calm, but pride got the better of her.

"What the hell is this?" Chelsea flung the note at Brandon. "Why did you write this?" She pointed at the offending note now on the ground.

"Oh, so now you *have time* to talk to me?" He didn't even bother to stop digging through his locker to look at her.

The heat rose in Chelsea's face. "I don't know what your problem is, Brandon. I'm trying to fix it, whatever *it* is."

"You never think of anyone else, Chelsea." Brandon took a deep breath. "You are always so busy, and *your busy* is more important than anyone else's *busy*. You didn't have time to talk to me, but you had time to talk to Lisa."

"I had to talk about my history project before golf. I was running late. I told you that."

Brandon's posture stiffened. "No, you decided I wasn't important enough to talk to. That's selfish. You think you're the center of the universe. You aren't, you know. Just because I like you doesn't mean you can treat me this way."

Chelsea wanted to roll her eyes. She didn't have time to ignore his feelings for her again. Every few months rumors would surface that Brandon liked her. And every few months she'd tell Brandon that she wasn't interested in dating. Anyone.

He turned to face her. "You are conceited and self-centered. You aren't the only one who is busy. You just get to pick and choose when you have time for me."

Chelsea's head swirled. She gasped for air. "But I—"

"No. You let me finish." His palm slammed into the metal lockers, and the sound crashed through the room. "You only have time for me when you need something from me, or you're bored.

No more. I'm done!" Brandon walked away.

The words stung worse than a slap. Chelsea slid down the wall and rested her chin on her bent knees. What just happened?

"What's Brandon's deal?" her sister asked as she entered the band locker room. "He stormed right past me, didn't even say hi." Tiff began to dig through her locker. When Chelsea didn't respond, Tiff finally noticed her on the floor. "Chelsea, are you okay? You look pale."

Chelsea fell back against the locker, clutching her chest. His words crushed her heart. She didn't just use him, did she? He was her best friend. He was the only one she could be herself with, and he thought her true self was selfish and self-centered.

The next day Chelsea overheard the conversations among their friends. "Who are we upset with? What did Brandon do? Why is Chelsea mad?" Their tight group of friends, including Joe, didn't know how to handle the situation. If it had been an actual break up of an actual relationship, people would have taken sides, and everyone could have moved on. But it wasn't that simple. There was no break, no rift, no fight.

When the nightly calls from Brandon had stopped, Chelsea figured it would last a week. When the second week rolled into the third, she wondered if he'd ever call. She resisted the urge to pick up the phone and call him herself. It was strange not hearing his voice, or his silly stories about what had happened at his job that day. His stories always made her smile, no matter how rough her day was at school.

When tears became a nightly ritual, Chelsea wondered what happened. She'd lost her best friend, her confidant, her flirt buddy, her security guard, her heart, and her sanity.

HOW I MET MY OTHER

Was she that selfish? She was always helping others, putting other people's needs before herself. She always gave her friends rides without asking for gas money or listened to them talk about their broken hearts when she should have been studying. Brandon had shown the world what he'd really thought of Chelsea. It was in black and white for everyone to see. Chelsea began to snap at her friends as a way of lashing out. No one wanted to be around her. She didn't even want to be around herself.

The cold silence between them continued. The spring band trip to Disneyland should have been the happiest time in the world, but it wasn't.

Tiff had been torn on who to spend the trip with. Chelsea had told her to go with Brandon. So, they spent their time going around Disneyland, having a blast, while Chelsea pretended to be happy and flirted with a boy she didn't even like in the hopes of making Brandon jealous. It went against everything Chelsea believed in. She just wanted Brandon back.

The bus ride home was quiet and still, in stark contrast to the celebratory mood going to California should have been. That suited Chelsea just fine. It gave her time to look over her *The House on Mango Street* homework. As she read Esperanza's struggles, it all became too much. Tears pooled and spilled onto the page. She tried to hold it in, but the tears refused to cooperate. The sound of crying filled the quiet bus.

Chelsea hung her head in despair. Tears dripped onto her lap. Time after time, she'd rejected him for one thing or another. Yes, she was lonely. And now she was selfish, too. Her sobs turned violent.

Chelsea could feel the eyes of those around her staring. How could she explain to them she was fine? She wasn't fine. She was tired, stressed, emotionally done.

Brandon was coming down the aisle, and she scrunched lower in her seat. If she were lucky, maybe the bus would swallow her whole.

Brandon slumped down in the empty seat next to her. "Are you okay?"

Her world spun out of control. She was losing all her friends, had lost him, and he was asking if she was okay?

Chelsea couldn't deal with this, with him, with everything she was feeling.

"We're not doing this now." Her voice gained strength. "Leave."

She wanted to look up, but kept her head down. He obeyed, but the anger permeated the distance between them.

He sent Tiff.

"Are you okay?" Tiff asked.

Chelsea didn't have the strength to respond in truth. "I'm fine. I don't have the energy to hash it all out right now, with all these people listening. Go ahead and go back. Tell him I'm fine."

Of course, she wasn't fine. He was everywhere. His presence in her life had threatened even her family's allegiances. Chelsea should have insisted that Tiff pick a side. She should have made her sister as miserable as herself. Chelsea sighed. Tiff was suffering as much as she was, if not more. Chelsea hated dragging everyone else into her own personal hell.

Chelsea had held her head high, pretended it didn't matter,

but her heart ached for the friendship she knew was gone. And over what? A misunderstanding that had blown out of proportion? She'd loved Brandon. But she hadn't been *in love* with him. At least that's what she always told herself.

Brandon had destroyed her image of herself, the kind, thoughtful, generous image she'd created. And the worst part was that Chelsea believed he was right. She'd been so busy trying to make her destiny and keep everyone out, everyone away to protect herself, that she hadn't seen how she'd hurt other people.

Someone had once told her. "*You* don't have to worry about a broken heart. You guard your heart so well, it will never be broken." How wrong that statement had been. Chelsea had guarded her heart, she'd guarded it well. She'd poke at the boys who had asked her out. She'd push their buttons to see how they'd respond. And they'd leave, move on to find their next crush. They never stuck around.

Except Brandon.

She'd pushed, she'd poked, she'd prodded. And when she hadn't been trying to push him away, he exploded, and exposed a part of Chelsea she wished to keep hidden from the entire world. Or at least from herself. And to what end? She was devastated, destroyed and for what? She'd protected her heart all right.

Chelsea had goals and a plan. She was too focused on taking on the world to allow herself to be heartbroken over a relationship. No one seemed to understand that.

As spring turned to summer, the depression and self-loathing seeped into every pore of her being. Did other people see her the same way he did?

Chelsea needed closure.

The opportunity soon presented itself. One afternoon Tiff rushed into the room. "I'm going to go get a smoothie with Brandon."

Tiffany was her sister, not his. He didn't need to check up on her. It was Chelsea's job to be the older sibling, not his.

"Are you asking or telling?" their mom said from the kitchen.

"Um, asking?"

"Okay."

Chelsea wasn't surprised at all by her mom granting Tiff permission. Everyone loved Brandon. He was still a part of the family.

Chelsea felt a burst of energy. She needed to change. Today was going to be the day. The cloud, the funk, the hell on earth that had been her life was going to end today.

Brandon pulled up in his white Ford truck. "You ready to go?" he asked Tiff as he avoided eye contact with Chelsea.

"Yep."

"I'm going too," Chelsea said.

"You're not invited," he said. Chelsea didn't care. She pushed her way into the back seat of his truck.

They drove in silence to the little bakery that sold smoothies on hot summer days.

Chelsea ordered a berry smoothie while Brandon and Tiff talked.

She sat down across from Brandon, took a deep breath and paused. She needed an excuse to talk to Brandon. Alone. "Tiff, I need you to go get me some napkins."

Brandon put his head down on the table. "No."

"Tiff go get me some napkins," she said. Tiff glared at her. She glared back.

As Tiff stomped away, Chelsea took a deep breath to settle her nerves. It was now or never. "Look at me." Her heart pounded.

She lifted Brandon's chin until they saw eye to eye. She paused. "I'm sorry. I'm sorry I hurt you and took your friendship for granted. I want to be friends again."

Chelsea could see her pain echoed in his eyes. She dropped his chin. Was he as miserable as she was? He hid his head in the crook of his arm. "Okay."

"What?" she asked. She needed to know that he forgave her.

"Yes, I accept your apology."

A sense of peace flooded her. She grabbed her smoothie and took a long drink. Chelsea tried not to flinch from the brain freeze that always came when she drank cold things too fast.

She was devastated by the cold void, more painful than any brain freeze, that had grown between them. Chelsea didn't like the type of person Brandon thought she was. She was going to prove that it wasn't true, that she'd changed. At least they were almost back on speaking terms. There was a frozen tundra of hurt feelings, but at least the sun promised to come out again. It was a good place to *restart*.

Their friendship healed and found a new normal. As their high school experience ended, Brandon asked Chelsea to go with him to the old car museum that friends of his family owned. It was a peace offering of sorts, a final hurrah before their lives went separate ways.

Chelsea felt the importance of this outing in the depths of her soul. It was going to change the course of her life. If nothing else, it would give her back her Brandon, her best friend. At worst, it would be goodbye.

He showed up in his truck. They'd spent so many hours driving around doing nothing in that truck.

Before *The Fight*, things had been different. Before *The Fight*, they had been inseparable. And on one occasion, Chelsea's mind went in a different direction.

It had been a strange evening, the night of the basketball game. The varsity boys' basketball team was having a stellar year, and the whole band was asked to play at the basketball game. Chelsea had arrived early for once and walked into an almost empty band room and found a guy changing his shirt. Her heart had skipped a beat. She couldn't tear her eyes from the sculpted Adonis in the instrument room. As his shirt went over his head, Chelsea's heart flipped in her chest. It was Brandon. Brandon wasn't allowed to look that way. Chelsea felt her life shift slightly to the left.

"Hey!" Brandon's cheerful voice had pulled Chelsea to reality again.

"Hey." Her voice sounded hollow.

"You okay?"

"What?" Her brain scrambled to find logic for what she was feeling. None came. "Yeah, I'm fine."

HOW I MET MY OTHER

"*Do you want a ride down to the gym?*" *The excitement in his voice was almost too much.* "*My dad let me bring the red truck tonight.*"

It wasn't that far, but Chelsea wasn't feeling right. What was that feeling? Was it attraction? To Brandon? But that couldn't be. He waited for her answer.

"*Sure.*"

"*Are you sure you're okay?*" *The concern in his voice was too much. She didn't have time to analyze her feelings. She didn't have time to take the focus off her goals. She didn't want a relationship with Brandon. He was her best friend. He was safe. They were safe.*

Chelsea nodded her head in agreement as she grabbed her trombone from her locker and followed Brandon to the truck. He sang along to Doo Wah Diddy Diddy as it played over the truck's radio.

"*I didn't know you liked classics,*" *she said.*

"*Of course. That's why they're called classics.*"

He blushed as he sang, "*Wedding bells are going to chime.*"

Her stomach continued spinning out of control. When they arrived at their destination, Chelsea shook her arms to get rid of the goosebumps as she hopped out and grabbed her trombone. "*Thanks for the ride.*"

Her world was never quite at equilibrium after that night. Then *The Fight* started. Now they were moving forward in an uncertain direction.

Chelsea got in the front seat of Brandon's truck and rolled down the window. She stuck her hand out and played with the wind as it ran through her fingers. Maybe today could be like it had been before *The Fight*.

Brandon pulled into the parking lot of the car museum. Chelsea decided she wouldn't let a dark thought of the past cloud her mind. Today was going to be a day of firsts or a day of lasts, but it wasn't going to be a day of pasts. Sitting on the swings in the front of the car museum and talking like the old days seemed as natural as breathing. The sun beat down on her and Brandon as they swung.

"Are you scared?" Chelsea asked and dragged her feet in time with the pendulum motion of the swing.

Brandon twisted back and forth in his own swing. "I guess so." He drew something in the sand with his foot but erased it. She wished erasing the past was that easy.

"I'm glad we're friends again." She grabbed hold of his swing. "Let's always be friends. Let's never fight over nothing again." She took a breath to settle her racing heartbeat. "Are you excited about college?" Her words sounded brittle as they came out of her mouth.

"I guess so."

"I'm going to Tech you know. It's only an hour away from Albuquerque." She would be like all the other freshman there, ready to grow up, eager to put her mark on the world. She'd get her degree in chemical engineering and then take on the corporate world.

"Any plans after college?" He pulled her swing towards him.

Her heart pounded faster. "Oh sure, I have big plans," she said. "I'm going to be the CEO of a Fortune 500 company by the time I'm thirty-five."

Could she live a life Brandon wasn't part of? He'd always been there, like a safe, cuddly teddy bear radiating strength, but one that she kept at arm's length. Who was she kidding? Brandon had never been at arm's length. Not once, not since the first time she gave the boy in the red flannel jacket a ride home after school their freshman year. No, he had always been there, always protecting her. Chelsea felt her world tilting again.

"So, you aren't going to have a family? Get married and all that?" he asked.

Chelsea squirmed in her swing. She wanted him in her life. She needed him in her life. But she needed him far away. He was already too much of a distraction. "Are you really going to move to New York and become a famous chef?"

"There's nothing for me here. No reason to stay."

His words were a punch to her heart. She gripped her swing tighter. Wasn't *she* reason enough to stay? But they weren't anything. Not really. They were just barely friends again. She couldn't—wouldn't—put herself out there.

"Are you going to do some school here and then move?" Hot tears pricked her eyes, forcing her to keep them down. "Or are you gone as soon as summer is over?"

"I might get a few basics out of the way before I go."

He was going to be here, even if just for the summer. Her lungs ached. She let out the breath she was holding and gripped her swing tighter. "That'll be nice. Maybe we can see each other some before you leave."

Brandon didn't say anything.

The silence lingered for an uncomfortable amount of time, then Brandon asked, "Why do you think you never had a boyfriend? Why didn't you ever ask anyone out?"

"Because my mom would have killed me if she discovered I asked someone out." Chelsea dragged her feet in the dirt. "I don't know. I suppose none of them were right for me. I always figured that if someone were really interested in me, they would stick around after I bruised their fragile male ego."

"So, it's better being friends than being your boyfriend?" Brandon asked.

Chelsea turned her swing in circles. "I guess so. If someone can't stand me at my best, how is he going to deal with me at my worst?" Brandon was the one person Chelsea had let see her best and worst side. Dizzy, she put her feet on the ground.

"So, you ended up with a lot of friends and no boyfriends?"

Chelsea nodded. "Yep. Just like you. We're friends again. And we're going to stay friends."

He grunted his agreement.

Friends couldn't hurt her any worse than she'd already been hurt by him. If that was what having a boyfriend was like, maybe she wasn't interested. They would need to be friends, and she would need to keep her distance. That night Chelsea had a hard time falling asleep.

"What are you doing?" A voice asked Chelsea. It wasn't any

voice. It was Joe, her friend and advisor. Joe had lobbied the hardest for her and Brandon to patch things up during The Fight.

She lay in the grass looking up at the sky. There were no clouds, and she felt a great loss. Brandon wasn't next to her. She looked around, but he was nowhere around. "What do you mean, what am I doing?"

"Why isn't he here with you? Looking up at the clouds?" Joe crossed his arms. He always did that when he had a point to make. "You need to tell him you love him."

"Love who?" Chelsea knew he was talking about Brandon.

"Why are you playing dumb? You love him. You've always loved him."

Chelsea laughed. "Of course I love him."

"Not like a friend," Joe interrupted. "You're in love with Brandon. If you don't tell him now, you're going to lose him."

"I have time."

"Do you? Are you sure he's going to keep waiting for you? Isn't four years long enough? Do you want him to find someone else? Will it make you happy for him to end up happy and you alone, with your high-power job and an empty house? Do you want to be the cool aunt that never had any kids, but took on the corporate world? With nothing to show but a big bank account?"

"I'm not going to end up alone. Brandon can never be more than my friend."

"And is friendship enough? If you lose Brandon's heart, you lose his friendship. You have to tell Brandon you love him."

The morning after their talk on the swings the whizzing sound of the alarm clock drew Chelsea from her sleep. She rubbed the sleep from her eyes and made her way to the kitchen as she did on most mornings. She hoisted herself up on the counter as her dad made breakfast.

"Daddy?"

"Yes, my girl?"

"I just woke up from the strangest dream."

"Oh?"

"I had a dream that Joe told me I was in love with Brandon. Is it possible for me to be in love with Brandon?"

He walked over and kissed his daughter on the forehead. "How do you feel about it?"

"I don't know. Confused? Joe is always right. But it just doesn't make sense. How can I love someone who hurt me so deeply?"

"Did he though?"

"No." She shook her head. "No. Brandon has never hurt me. Not intentionally. He's always done just the opposite. He spoiled me when I needed spoiling, like with those Phantom of the Opera tickets and flowers that everyone pitched a fit over after my knee surgery. He's always been there."

"Is it possible for you to be in love with Brandon? That's up to you to decide." He turned back to making breakfast. "Now tell me about that dream."

"Someone told me I had to tell Brandon I loved him. I can't be in love with Brandon. I just can't."

He put down his spatula "Why not?"

"It's Brandon. He's like a brother to me. I can't be in love my brother. Well, he's not a *real* brother. I guess there's no good reason why I can't love him. I have this feeling that I need to tell Brandon I love him, but I'm scared. I don't want to fall in love. If I fall in love, then how do I know if it's real or not? I don't want to get hurt."

Her dad hugged her as tears flowed down her face. "It's part of growing up and a natural part of life. When you get married and have a little girl, your heart will break when she falls in love and you'll tell her it's part of growing up." He wiped the tears from her eyes. "It's okay. It's the way things are supposed to be."

Chelsea rubbed her sternum. She didn't like this part of growing up. "Do I have to?"

"Yes."

"Do you like Brandon, Dad?"

"What? Are you kidding? Don't you know we've been conspiring together for years?" His laughter filled the kitchen. "Didn't I always tell you that your knight in shining armor would ride up on a white steed? Maybe I got it wrong. Maybe it was a white pick-up truck instead."

After four years of friendship and pushing him away, how was she going to finally tell Brandon how she felt?

Moving day arrived. Chelsea offered to help Brandon move his family's things from their house in town to their new home in the mountains. They packed Brandon's truck to the brim with boxes and Chelsea's jeep as well. They dropped their load off at the new house and started to head back for another load. Chelsea threw her keys to Tiff and hopped into the truck with Brandon.

As Brandon merged onto the freeway, Chelsea gathered her gumption. After all, Brandon driving down the freeway at 75 miles an hour while he pulled a trailer seemed like the perfect time to confess.

Maybe this wasn't such a good idea. It would change everything. "Brandon," Chelsea said.

"Yes?"

"I've got something to tell you." She took a deep breath in hopes that her voice wouldn't sound shaky. "I kinda like you, and I've decided you can ask me out now."

The truck swerved. Chelsea grabbed onto the truck's door handle for support.

"What?" Brandon regained control of the truck. "I don't think I heard you right."

"I said you can ask me out now."

"Do you think it's the best time for this conversation?" Brandon asked. There was exasperation with a tinge of hope in his voice. It tickled her heart.

Chelsea let go of the handle. "I thought it would be better to tell you while you were distracted."

Brandon sighed. Perhaps it was just exasperation. "I've liked you for four years, and you decided to tell me I can ask you out while I was distracted?"

Her heartbeat sped up. Chelsea tried not to smile. "Yep."

Brandon sighed again. "So, do you want to go out with me?"

Chelsea played with her ponytail and checked her mirror for traffic. She didn't want to get into an accident if he overreacted. "It's a family rule." She wasn't being dramatic, she just wasn't sure how to tell him. She tried not to smile. "You have to ask my dad for permission first."

They could date. They *should* date. That's all her heart could think about. Friends were good. Friends were safe. Friends would always be there for one another. But a soulmate would go beyond safe to create a new life. And Chelsea was starting to see what a life with Brandon would be like. Brandon would be there for her even if things spun out of control, again.

It had started innocently enough. And it would end just the same.

Get an update on Chelsea and Brandon and see pictures at www.orangeblossombooks.com

How Funny It Was:

Part One

Cute Hat Boy and the Weird Girl

The Story of Paige and Matt

Year: 2009
By Paige Lavoie

"How do you eat an artichoke?" I shout into the phone. I don't even open with "Hello" or "How's it going?"—just launch right into the question as soon as the call is answered. I need advice, and I need it quick. Why I am screaming about produce on the phone, you might ask?

Cute Hat Boy. That might sound silly, but it's not. This is serious business. ULTRA-serious business, in fact, and to understand this to the fullest extent, we're going to have to go back a few months. Our story starts at a cozy coffee shop in Orlando named "Natura."

I'm looking frantically around the coffee house when I catch a glimpse of my friend Jessi's spiky brown hair, bouncing up and down as she flails around, trying to wave me over to the other side of the shop. She's shorter than I am, so all I can make out is a blur of hair and black-jelly-bracelet arms until I make my way through the crowd to where she's standing.

Jessi, much like everyone else in Natura, is objectively too cool to be my friend. We met during Universal Studios' Halloween Horror Nights, and I've been driving an hour from Disney to the University of Central Florida to watch her rock out on her ukulele ever since.

The coffee house is long and narrow. It has quirky local art, including paper mâché dinosaur bones mounted on the wall, which makes you feel like you're an extra in a movie. Tonight it's a sardine-tin-level crowd full of indie rock kids. Cases for the hodge-podge of instruments are stacked up by the stage, right next to where Jessi is still flailing. Inching through the crowd, I accidentally step on or elbow everyone in my path. My twin sister, Lily, on the other hand, has no problem getting to the front of the line. She orders for me, and I slip her some cash. She knows the drill by now. I hate talking to people.

As I'm waiting for my drink, I notice a boy smiling across the room, shooting arrows through my heart. I'm not the type to get overwhelmed by smiles from cute strangers, but I've seen this boy before—so often, in fact, that I secretly call him "Cute Hat Boy." The "cute" part is self-explanatory. He has giant puppy-dog eyes and a glittering smile, dimples included. His shoulders are the kind you wish you could snuggle right into. The "hat" part refers to the fact that he always wears the best hats: hand-painted top hats, fuzzy knitted caps, even bowler hats like the one he's sporting today.

Unfortunately, his smile isn't directed at me. My heart aches as I watch him chatting animatedly with a cute girl holding a ukulele.

Lily hands me my drink before disappearing into the crowd to hang out with her friends. This place is nuts. Just looking around is gives me anxiety. "There's nowhere to sit," I complain as people squeeze past us. Heck, there's nowhere to stand.

"Nah, it's fine," Jessi says confidently, plopping down on the coffee table already cluttered with coffee cups and a hookah the customers before us abandoned. She points to the old guitar case next to her.

"Neither of these are chairs," I say, but she just shrugs. Natura is Jessi's second home, so she'd know better than I would. The edges of the case are duct-taped together, and there's a giraffe painted on the front. Carefully, I sit down. Everything Jessi owns is customized in some way. Her notebook of song lyrics is made from old cereal boxes, and there are scribbles on her shoes.

"You sure this is okay?" I ask again. I don't want to ruin her guitar case.

"Yeah, don't worry about it."

But it's me, and I worry about everything. I sit lightly on the case—it's honestly not very comfortable, but it gets me slightly out of the way of the crowd coming and going from the shop. I take a deep breath and a sip of my Boba tea. The sugary honeydew flavor hurts my teeth but tastes good. People flutter around everywhere. With the constant motion it's almost hard to focus on the conversation Jessi and I are having. Then suddenly her head jerks up to look at someone.

HOW I MET MY OTHER

I follow her eyes, panic rising in my chest.

Cute Hat Guy stands like two feet from me. Why is he standing right here? And oh my God, why is he looking at me? And why is he so much cuter up close? His brown hair is a little shaggy, and it looks impossibly soft. I try (and fail) not to stare like a weirdo.

"Is this okay?" Jessi points to the guitar case, and I suddenly realize this guitar case was never hers.

No.

Nope.

I'm sitting on the cute boy's guitar case. This is the worst moment of my life.

I watch his adorable face twist into a hesitant expression, like he's trying to figure out a polite response. But here I am, a total stranger, sitting right on his musical instrument.

"Yeah...just don't—" he begins, then starts shifting his weight from side to side.

Just don't what?

Just don't crush his guitar?

Does this mean he thinks I'm fat?

No way. A normal-sized person could totally crush a guitar case.

Wait, could they? Oh my god. He thinks I'm fat.

The cute boy thinks I'm fat.

I need to leave. I need to go home. Tonight is cursed, and I can feel my face getting redder as he stands there and stares at me with his big, pretty eyes.

I open my mouth to speak, but words are so not a thing right now. And considering my current train of thought, maybe it's better that way. I imagined trying to start a conversation with him dozens of times, but how could anyone bounce back from this? No conversation in history is ever going to go:

"Hey, how did you meet your husband?"

"Oh, I almost crushed his guitar with my butt."

Did I really just daydream about marrying Cute Hat Boy? I need to get a grip. *Get a freaking grip, Paige.* I need to do something...anything! But I'm too late. Once I snap myself out of it, Matt has already vanished into the crowd before I even have a chance to apologize.

"Oh hey, it looks like there are little stackable chairs in the back." Jessi points to a stack of small stools in the corner. I'm mortified that we're just noticing this now.

We grab some chairs, and she plops them right in front of the stage. I've never sat this close. I'm more of a sit-in-a-dark-corner-and-hope-no-one-notices-me kind of girl. But it's fine.

This night can't possibly get more awkward.

"Next up, we have Matt in the Hat!"

Well, I was wrong. Cute Hat Boy—a.k.a. Matt—is now on stage, and he's wearing a freaking harmonica around his neck.

He strums his unscratched guitar and starts the first song. Okay, I need to play it cool. Don't smile like a weirdo, but also don't glare at him, I try to tell myself. I keep my lips in a neutral position, and Jessi leans over.

"He's just adorable," she says in a tone reserved for talking about puppies and younger brothers.

"Yeah," I agree quietly. He's so close that if I'm any louder, he might hear me. He's only a few feet away, and at the same time, entirely out of reach.

His big eyes look up, and for a moment they're locked on mine. I panic and try my best to maintain my neutral expression. He nervously fumbles with his guitar pick, and it slides out of his hand and clicks across the stage. Everyone laughs, including him. There's something carefree about the way he pulls out another guitar pic and starts again. I watch his every move on stage—he's filled with charisma and nervous energy, and something about the way he sings makes everyone around him smile. It's goofy and fun, and with every second I like him more.

I get home past midnight and eat freezer pizza in front of my laptop, which isn't an untypical way for me to spend the wee hours of the morning. But tonight, tonight I had a mission: Internet-stalking the man formerly known as "Cute Hat Boy." Just who was Matt in the Hat? And why did it feel like my heart had been run over by a bulldozer?

"He doesn't think you're fat," my mom's voice chimes from across the kitchen—she has listened to this story about three times since I got home, and is now doing lunges in the kitchen.

"He thought my giant butt was going to crush his guitar." I roll my eyes and turn my attention back to the computer.

"He was probably just intimidated by your beauty. You get it from your mom." She scoops up our Yorkshire terrier, Tinkerbelle, and uses her as a weight. Tink seems more interested in my pizza to be honest but allows herself to be turned into a canine piece of exercise equipment with no reaction whatsoever.

"Mom—"

"We have good genes—look at your Grandma!" she continues while Tinkerbelle begins to wiggle away from her arms in an attempt to get closer to the pizza on my plate. She's right. No matter how good our "genes" are, it doesn't change the fact that he's the cute boy, and I am, and forever will be, the weird girl. I may have gotten my Grandma's cheekbones, but I have 0% of her charm.

Mom is finally asleep when, after searching through every Top 8 on MySpace, I spot his picture, and a pair of doe-like brown eyes stare back at me. I click on his profile, eager for details! Is he dating anyone? What kind of music does he like? I want to know everything, but I totally feel like a stalker.

My heart pounds with every second as I scroll down his page.

Matt in the Hat. Single. Oh, thank God.

I read every detail on his profile, and learn that not only is he cute, but he also seems pretty funny. (And looks really good in a pirate costume.)

We'd barely spoken, online or in person. I am sitting in front of my computer with sweaty palms, overthinking every little sentence when my friend request is followed by a sheepish "Hey." We somehow get onto the topic of pillow forts, because duh, pillow forts are amazing.

"I haven't made a pillow fort in forever," he messages. Is this an invitation?

"Haha me neither," I type back

"We should make one sometime." If it wasn't an invitation before it 100% is now.

We pick a day. Just two strangers making a pillow fort. It's totally-probably-maybe not a date. There's nothing to worry about—at least that's what I keep telling myself until my phone rings. Matt is calling me on the phone. Ahhh!

There is one thing I am more uncomfortable with than talking to people in person, and it's talking to people on the phone.

"He's calling me," I shout, staring down at his pixelated name.

"Answer it," Lily's voice shouts back from the kitchen. I shut the door to my room before anyone has a chance to eavesdrop.

"Hello?" I answer, in a tone way higher than my actual voice.

"Hi. It's Matt." His voice comes through the speaker, and I'm instantly swooning until I realize the only reason people call before plans is to cancel them. I brace myself for disappointment.

"I was just wondering, have you had dinner? I have these great artichokes I need to use. I was thinking about steaming them."

Hold up, how fancy is this guy? Steamed artichokes? I've only ever had artichoke dip before.

"Sure, um that would be great," I answer, pacing around my room. My chest is tight, and I can feel the color draining from my face. He's making me dinner.

He's actually making me dinner. I pull myself together to finish our conversation, and as soon as we hang up, I call the one person I know with more answers than Google itself: My best friend, Meaghan.

"How do you eat an artichoke?" I scream.

And that is how I ended up here, on the phone with Meaghan, shouting about artichokes and generally panicking. Because hello: how can I have any chill? I literally never thought this would happen in a million years.

"I have no idea," she replies without skipping a beat. I hear her typing. "Wikihow says,

Gently nibble or scrape off the tender bits of the bottom of the leaf by putting the leaf in your mouth, closing your teeth on it, and pulling the leaf outwards. Weird. Hey, why do you need to know how to—"

"HE IS MAKING DINNER," I scream, flopping onto my bed.

"OH MY GOSH!" She's heard about the pillow fort plans, but this is big news.

"Okay, okay, it's fine. It's not like it's a date," I say, trying to keep myself calm.

"If he's making you food, it's a date!"

"OH MY GOD IT'S A DATE."

I change outfits three times before I finally land on a black and white gingham dress. I look at the clock—I don't like driving on highways. Actually, I don't like driving at all. I only ever go to the university side of town if I can bum a ride off someone—normally Lily.

But this is a date with Matt. *The* Matt. I have to go, even if it means a million back roads and shortcuts. It can't add that much time to my commute, can it?

HOW I MET MY OTHER

I pull up to his apartment complex three hours late. No one would smile at a girl three hours late for a date—but there's Matt, waving and smiling as he walks out to greet me.

He's taller than I remember and wearing his cute knit hat and a blue shirt with a ramen noodle monster on the front. It's the most casual I've ever seen him look, which makes me realize this is the first time we've ever really hung out. We've barely said three or four sentences in person to each other before, and now we're about to spend an entire evening together. The thought makes my stomach jolt. I've never been alone in a boy's apartment before.

Much like how I have no experience eating artichokes, I also have very little experience dating—actually, more like none whatsoever.

There are several foods I would never want to eat in front of a boy I like. Corn on the cob? Not date food. Burritos? No, thank you. But, pulling off leaves of an artichoke and having to scrape the meat off with my teeth? Yeah, artichokes are maybe not a great date food either. And what was I supposed to talk about?

His roommate's adorable Shetland sheepdog, Cider, runs around us. He seems to adore Matt. That's a good sign. Dogs are a good judge of character. I should have brought Tink along as a second opinion, but knowing her, she'd be more interested in the food.

Ah, the food. It's apparent he has gone all out. He even, impressively, manages to keep everything warm, and nothing is overcooked, considering I was three hours late.

Matt has prepared pasta with peppers and sausage, rosemary potatoes, and...

The artichokes.

(Cue the dramatic music.)

They sit in the center of the table, with a bowl next to them to put the discarded leaves in, and another bowl with olive oil and seasoning.

"They're a lot of work, but that's part of why they're fun. My dad would make them for family dinners. It's probably the fanciest thing I know how to make," Matt says shyly.

Up until this point, I wasn't even sure if he was interested or not. But you don't make a girl you just like as a *friend* the fanciest thing you know how to cook, do you? My chest flutters with nerves, and I cover my mouth with my hand as I eat. I hate eating around people. What if he thinks I'm gross?

"You don't have to cover your mouth while you eat," he says, but I've committed, and I'm also 99% sure I've smeared my red lipstick onto my chin in the process of scraping the artichoke meat off the leaves. The conversation is awkward and giggly, and with every passing comment, I'm worried about what we'll talk about next. At the same time, I'm having fun—a lot of fun. I've liked Matt from afar for months. It's a little scary that up close, I like him much more. Still, I'm worried. What will the "thing" be that makes me less cool and likable in his eyes?

"Ready to make our fort?" he asks once we're finished eating. It was also part of the plan to make baked goods, so I've brought over a box mix of cinnamon streusel muffins, but those are for later.

Build the fort. Make snacks. Eat said snacks in the fort. A foolproof plan.

The blankets were already gathered, and together we steal

every available pillow in the house. In his room, he has an old bunk bed frame covered in bottle caps and draped with a hammock, which makes for a pretty good base.

A dog snout snuffles past the sheet. "Oh no! We're under attack!" Matt exclaims, pulling pillows off his bed to fill in the gaps left in the blankets. "We have to reinforce our structures!" He's goofy, and it just makes him cuter. Everything he does turns me into human-shaped Jell-O, and there's no cure.

We're laughing, but it's darker now—and somehow that makes things seem a little more serious. He pulls out his guitar and starts to strum a little, smiling.

As I feel myself start to melt, panic ensures. How am I going to form complete sentences with my brain so fuzzy?

"Do you play?" Matt asks.

Oh, no. Come on, brain, be useful. "No...um, I used to take lessons—I play the bass, but I'm not very good," I manage to stammer out.

"Here." He swivels the guitar around so his hands are still around its neck, but I'm able to reach around the body. We're closer than we've ever been before.

One hand forms the chords of the song *Brown-Eyed Girl* while his other hand is on top of mine, guiding me to strum along with the melody. The song ends, and we both lean forward.

Everything feels like it's in slow motion—and yet, it's moving fast. Every second that passes our faces are just a little closer together, breath entangling until finally our lips touch. The kiss is soft at first. His lips press against mine, and I can't believe any of this is happening. I am in a pillow-fort, kissing the freaking guy of my dreams.

Oh, my gosh we're kissing.

This is a big deal! I don't want to stop but at the same time...

"We shouldn't kiss too much," I say suddenly.

Matt backs up a little and looks at me. "Okay...why not?"

"Because if we kiss too much, you'll get bored."

"I'll get bored of kissing you?"

"Yeah." It feels kind of silly to hear out loud, but it doesn't change my anxiety. If he kisses me too much tonight, why would he ever want to kiss me again?

He looks at me with certainty in his eyes, a small laugh escaping his lips.

"That's not possible."

Get an update on Paige and Matt and see pictures at www.orangeblossombooks.com

Eddie and Me

The Story of Bob and Eddie
Year: 1988
By Robert Bellam

How do you rationalize the concept of commitment after being abandoned by another? I'd spent sixteen years of my life in a relationship that ended when I was 46—damaged, withdrawn, and none-the-wiser.

This new fear became my routine, joining other fears like ski lifts, mountain tops, or the simple act of climbing a tree. I felt I'd never be free to stand on that mountaintop, every day, alongside a man who could love me back. The rejection made me spend more than a few months alone before I could begin to venture out into the world beyond my living room.

During this downtime, I wasn't interested in replacing one failed relationship with another. The singular encounters that occurred during this period were short-lived, often measured by the simple tick-tock of the pendulum in a tall case clock. This way of living was not always pretty or satisfying, but it was mine.

Still, it left me unfulfilled.

HOW I MET MY OTHER

Everything changed one sweltering summer day in 1988 when I was asked to go on a Baltimore Harbor "Leather Cruise to Nowhere" in support of an AIDS Benefit for a group my County Health Department had funded. I was the agency's AIDS Information Manager, responsible for codifying a program to train speakers for Health Fairs, public groups, and other outreach opportunities to present an accurate message about the then current HIV/Aids epidemic in the LGBTQ community.

The afternoon before leaving, I showered, shaved, and spritzed my favorite Givenchy's Imperial Cologne in all the right places. I already had a fresh haircut and I carefully dressed. With armor in place, my co-workers and I downed a drink or two before leaving for the boat. I was fortified but not emotionally prepared for anything beyond, at best, a one-night stand.

Once on board the ship, the group huddled together. With our new drinks in hand, all of us scanned the crowd. I was the only single person in the group. Jason, my friend and co-worker, turned to me and asked, "Bob, why don't you go and check out the scene? Who knows, you might meet someone tonight."

I shrugged, not happy with the suggestion. I didn't know how to tell him, *No, I'd rather stay here with you guys.*

Inside, I knew my friend was right. This was a party. I'd been to them before and was usually successful at not committing myself to anyone who came on to me. After all, I was the responsible one and still in control.

I smiled then shrugged, "Why not? I'll just look around for a bit. Who knows, you may be right."

Though I was nervous, I left the safety of my friends behind and wandered through the decks and public areas until I discovered the dance floor. It was crowded. People swaying in time to the music, their arms in the air, hips gyrating. The air pulsed with the beat of the music. This was the life I'd known before: happy people savoring each wonderful moment life had to offer. I grinned like a fool, even shuffled my feet in response to the rhythms. I loved it.

The boat was impossibly hot and humid. Sweat dripped from my body in the tight unairconditioned enclosure. I took a sip from my drink and quickly searched through the faces on the dance floor to see if I knew anyone.

Amongst them, standing under a spotlight, was a man. He was blond, had a great body, and the most beautiful, sparkling blue eyes I'd ever seen.

In my mind, I imagined a higher power shining this intense beam on him, just for me. The light was powerful enough to pull me towards him, to charm and attract me like a flute would charm a cobra in a basket.

Based on his jerky dance moves, he was no Fred Astaire, but I didn't care. His dance partner was a gorgeous black woman, tall and elegant. Being the blockhead I am, the thought he might be straight, married to her, or have a partner never entered my mind.

I just wanted to be with him, even if it meant I might only have one chance to dance with this incredible stranger. Without stopping to think that perhaps this might be a bad idea, I edged across the floor, skirted between twisting bodies, and said, "Excuse me, excuse me, pardon me."

At last, I stood directly behind the woman. Tapping her lightly on the shoulder, I asked, "Do you mind if I cut in?"

God, that was so lame. My cheeks flamed red, but I couldn't stop there.

They both stopped dancing and stared at me as if they were fish flapping on a boat. It seemed as if everything had come to a halt, the music, the heat, the background noises while I waited. After undergoing several nervous heartbeats, she paused, turned to this blond god, and asked, "What do you think, do you want to dance with him?"

He mumbled a few words I couldn't hear. She smiled, nodded at me, and left. The next thing I knew we were dancing and I couldn't keep my eyes off him. The musicians were still playing the same song, and we promptly moved in our imitation of what might pass for dancing.

I said, "Hi, I'm Bob what's your name?"

"Eddie."

"What do you do?" I asked.

"Direct Mail Marketing, you?"

"I work in Public Health."

"Is she waiting for you, was she your date?"

"No, I asked her to dance with me."

I couldn't believe how good this made me feel. Eight little words had reassured me. "Great, I'm happy I cut in. Now, I don't have to worry about her feelings."

"No, I think she'll be fine. But, you did come on a little strong. You're kind of intimidating," he said.

His comment bruised my ego. "Me, intimidating? No way. I'm just here to enjoy myself, and I'm glad I've met you. If you feel threatened, I can leave. But I'd rather we go to the bar and get another drink. Personally, I'd rather have a drink with you than go anywhere else."

Oh God, I was on the ropes and becoming defensive. Here I was chasing after someone when I didn't know if he had any interest in me. All my issues about abandonment, anger, rejection, and loss swirled in my brain. Maybe leaving my friends wasn't such a clever idea after all.

Eddie relaxed then smiled. "A drink would be great. But let's talk about something else. Like the weather, books, anything."

I suspected this assignation was over and became suspicious he wasn't sure what to do next. For the moment, I'd have to stop any subtle attempts to pick him up. At the bar, his eyes kept darting from left to right, obviously, searching for an escape route. "You, look nervous, are you sure we're good? I'd like to have a drink with you, but if you don't, I'll understand."

He ran his fingers through his hair. "Yeah, yeah...I'm okay. Just searching for an exit in case we have to get out of here in a hurry."

"Wow, you're fast on your feet." What did it all mean? I forged ahead. "You know, I like your one-liners, they're funny. I think you have a great sense of humor. You have more going on than just your beautiful blue eyes."

Those eyes brightened. Was it with interest? He said, "Thanks for that, but sometimes people think there's an edge to the things I say. But, that's just the way I am. Anyway, I'm glad you think I'm funny."

He didn't run away. Instead, we drank and talked about

ourselves and our interests. We began with what our jobs were like, the recent movies or plays we'd seen. Then on to the actors, actresses we liked, where we'd traveled, and more. I was enjoying myself and by this time feeling rather frisky from the alcohol.

It still had not occurred to me to find out if he was straight, bi, etc.

It was 2:00 a.m. and when the boat docked, I couldn't find my friends on the pier. Later, I learned they had seen me with him earlier and left. I stepped off the gangplank, a cloud of happiness surrounding me.

Eddie faced me and said, "Now, what do I do with you?"

"What was that?" I asked.

He repeated, "Now what do I do with you?"

Not the most romantic thing I've ever been told, but worse things have been said to me. He turned his back, and I whispered, "My God, he's straight! But surely he might lean in the other direction."

I used my most helpless and endearing voice, "I don't have my car here at the pier, it's at my friend's house. I don't see them anywhere and I'll need a ride...wait, I have an idea! Why don't we go to my place in Washington, D.C.? We can come back tomorrow and get my car then."

Oh my God, that had to have been the worst pickup line in history. I was blatantly throwing myself at him. I blushed again. I was turning into a male whore. Please don't let him reach for his wallet and hand me two dollars.

Instead, he said, "No, I'm too tired to drive that far and then back. Why don't we get a motel room for the night?"

Could this be the moment? I smiled, "Yeah that would be great! We won't have to drive too far, so we'll be saving money on gas."

I can be such a genius at times. Eventually, we found a motel with a neon light flashing "Vacancy." It wasn't a pleasure palace, but rather kind of tired and sad. The paint on the building was a faded tan color, and a downspout was crushed from a car that must have backed over the curb and smashed into it. Next to the parking lot, there was a tiny pool so full of algae, you could almost walk across the surface. I hoped this wasn't a harbinger of things to come.

We pulled in and stopped at the office, which was apparently a half door under the portico. Within minutes the manager appeared at the Dutch Door, which for this place must be their registration desk. He just stood there in a stained tee shirt—I'm sure he'd seen this all before—then he growled at us, "Want a room? I have one available, but it only has a queen-sized bed in it. Thirty-five dollars for the night."

Eddie looked at me, and I looked at him, then I leaned over Eddie, "That's fine, we'll take it." I put my arm around him, "Pay the man, honey!" What can I say? I was pleasantly drunk.

Now it was Eddie's turn to be red-faced. The manager grunted, Eddie paid him the money, and he gave us the key.

We went in our room. It was just as tired as the building suggested, but it was to be our beautiful love nest! The ceiling had a bow in it, the curtains couldn't close all the way, and the putrid green carpet was smelly and horribly stained as if an irrepressible "Cat Lady" had been on a road trip with sixty of her favorite felines and then decided to spend three weeks in this room before moving on. I gagged and my stomach churned. The room spun around me. I was going to be sick and ran for the bathroom.

Nausea from the carpet and all the alcohol gripped my guts. I heaved. Between bouts of extreme esophageal contractions, I rested my forehead on the cold porcelain bowl for relief. I made a fool out of myself again. Eddie must be wondering, "What have I gotten myself into with this stranger? He's probably some back alley drunk who can't hold his liquor."

Finally, it was over. I showered, rinsed my mouth, and returned to the room. He was sound asleep. Ouch, he couldn't wait for me to come out. Lifting the covers to peek, I whispered, "You're still in your underwear."

This wasn't my first rodeo, and I wasn't feeling that great. Tomorrow was another day, another chance, and I decided I needed to lie down too. Throwing the towel aside, I jumped under the covers and draped my arm over his chest. He didn't flinch, not one quiver. I wondered if he was actually asleep or pretending. I allowed myself to succumb to Hypnos, the Greek god of dreams.

Later in the morning, the sun at its zenith, I woke up. Eddie had bought us coffee. Sweet. Those eyes were just as amazing in daylight as they had been last night. He surprised me when he put his coffee down and kissed me. I could taste sugar on his lips. He put his hand against my cheek. It was warm.

"Eddie, that was so sweet, how come such a nice guy like you hasn't been scooped up by now?"

He simply smiled.

I was happy and content, but not so sure about him, even with the sugary kiss. I hoped again that he might be gay or at least bi.

On the way to breakfast, he didn't talk much while I rambled on and on about anything that popped into my brain. He didn't respond to my babbling. Because of his silence, I suspected he might be having second thoughts about last night. Or, perhaps he still didn't know what to do with me. Usually after a one-night stand, there's a bond that forms between two people who party all night and then enjoy the morning together. I still wasn't sure how he felt.

In a restaurant, over Bloody Mary's, I decided to find out the truth. "So, where do you live?" I asked.

"On Duke street in Alexandria, Virginia. I have a condo there."

"I like Alexandria. It's a beautiful city." I dropped my gaze to my coffee cup and asked, "Are you married?"

"I'm divorced and have three children. They live in Florida. I miss them but get to see my kids every now and again. What about you?"

I couldn't answer. A once married man with children. Oh my. The nausea was coming back. Now, what would I do with *him*?

I was a gay man out with someone who had an ex-wife and children. Experience taught me these restraints meant no future for us if we were to move beyond a one-night thing. I'd been with men like him before, and it never worked out. Family was family, and there was no room for me in someone's family.

Unbelievable. I thought he might be sent from the heavens but this would be just another one-night stand.

To rush past this stumbling block, I shared my litany of past romantic failures. I wanted to establish some distance between us. He had shaken me to the core and I was so sick that I just wanted to leave.

We finished our breakfast, and it was time for him to say, *Thanks, it's been great, have a nice life.*

Instead, he asked, "I don't come to Baltimore often. But I love this city. Would you like to spend some time sightseeing? We can visit the Inner Harbor's shopping mall and the aquarium. There's also a hotel that has an outside elevator. We can ride to the top, it has a great view of this section of Baltimore. Want to do it?"

I frowned. His invitation was unsettling and I had to think. Did he want us to continue our date? I wasn't even sure if I wanted this relationship to go anywhere. I had an enjoyable time with him but was I ready for another relationship?

"That would be great, but are you positive you want to do this with me? It could be fun, I've only been in and out of the city for meetings and haven't seen much of it. But, I have to warn you, I'm wary of the hotel and not a fan of tall buildings," I said.

"Why not? Don't worry, there are glass walls, you can't fall out. Besides, the view is worth it, even if you do fall out!"

Lord have mercy. Those certainly were not the most comforting words but I did want to spend time with him. I studied my shoes, then said, "Can we save the hotel for later?"

"Of course, but you won't know what you're missing if we don't go there."

"Okay, I'll think about it. I just feel safer on the ground."

Our daytime adventure began. We went into the Harbor Mall, toured the shops, and talked to all the merchants we met. He later told me, "You know, I think you could carry on a conversation with a rock." Cute, huh?

He was a funny and interesting guy, who seemed to take pleasure in everything and saw things in a way I didn't. In the shops, he looked at statues and knickknacks and picked out the smallest detail, then pointed them out to me. It was fascinating the way his mind worked.

After the mall, Eddie and I stopped for hamburgers and downed a couple of ice cold beers at Hooters. Again with those incredible blue eyes, he said, "Let's drive around the city for a bit. There are some interesting statues and places we can see. Do you have time?"

"Yes, that would be great."

Eddie sure knew the city. We drove everywhere and saw almost everything it had to offer. I learned the Bromo Seltzer Tower in Baltimore had been used to drop molten lead from its top into sand at the base to form bullets. I never checked it out, but it seemed plausible.

It was getting dark when he said, "It's time for the hotel elevator. Are you game?"

How could I say no? It had been a wonderful day, and I didn't want it to end. We entered the lobby just as the sun was sinking below the horizon. The thought of an elevator—really a glass cage on rails—hanging on the side of a building made me sweat. Why on earth would anyone want to build such a thing?

We entered the lobby and faced the elevators. The doors opened, we stepped inside, and Eddie pressed the button. Just as I thought, it looked like a fragile thing, a glass coffin to bury us in if we were hit by anything.

I wanted a paper bag while we glided up through the atrium.

HOW I MET MY OTHER

We stared down at people moving in the lobby beneath our feet, then broke through to the night sky. My knees quivered.

"Look out the windows. It's incredible," Eddie said.

He was right. My eyes grew wide as I took in the brightly lit city, the harbor, the sky, the traffic under my feet. I was thunderstruck as the Baltimore Harbor spread out before us. Headlights from the passing cars and street lamps took my breath away alongside my dire thoughts of death and destruction.

I took Eddie's hand. "This is incredibly beautiful. It's the most amazing sight I've ever seen. Thank you for taking me here."

The ride was over too soon, but he asked, "Do you like Italian food? I know a place that's excellent and authentic. You'll like it."

"You're not going to believe it, but I don't want this to end just yet. I hope you're having as great a time as I am. You are, aren't you?" I said.

"Let's not get mushy. Let's go eat!"

In minutes we were in the Italian quarter of the city. We scanned sidewalk chalkboards outside several restaurants advertising specialties like poultry, bread, fresh vegetables, baked fish, pasta, risotto, bean dishes from Tuscany, Sicily, Genoa, and Bologna. The aromas of these foods wafted through the air. I was starving.

We went into his favorite one, ordered drinks, and looked at the menu. "Let's start with the Calamari as an appetizer and then either Veal Scaloppini or Pasta Primavera. Or, would you like something else?" he asked.

I didn't know what any of that was. As someone of Irish Catholic/Scandinavian descent, Italian food, other than spaghetti and meatballs, was foreign to me. He ordered. The food arrived, and we began to eat. "This is delicious," I said as I ate the calamari, "What is it? It looks like little octopuses."

"I'll tell you later."

"Is it that bad?"

"No, it's delicious, isn't it? Just keep eating. After the veal, I'll tell you."

When he finally told me what it was, I said, "You mean I ate squid!" I playfully put my finger down my throat. "Wait until I tell my mother."

After dinner, he drove me back to my friends' place and spent the night. We all slept in the same room, so it was a chaste evening for us. But we did listen to my friends passionately groan and moan while we giggled like teenagers under the covers.

In the morning, we exchanged phone numbers and dated off and on for a couple of months. I liked being with him and he was getting serious about the relationship. There were trips to the beach, dinners out, flowers, and gifts—everything I could ask for. Still, I was afraid of committing because I had been hurt too badly in the past.

We went back to Baltimore in the fall to see *The Unsinkable Mollie Brown* with Debbie Reynolds. This time we stayed at a better hotel, with a view of the harbor. After dinner, we returned to the room.

"This room doesn't have the best view of the river." Eddie smiled. "Why don't you fix a drink and I'll open the window so we can take in the night sky."

I think we were on the twenty-sixth floor and a ledge ran

around the building. I filled two glasses with ice and poured a good amount of scotch. We watched the traffic below and the planes leaving the airport. The harbor was to our left and the night sky filled with brilliant stars while we drank.

My defenses were breaking down. Eddie was the kindest man I'd met in a long time, and I was still confused about my feelings. He didn't place demands on me, and I could be myself. What was wrong with me?

"Eddie, tonight is feeling incredibly special. The play was great, and dinner too. We do have a wonderful time when we're together, don't we?"

"I know, Bob, we're good together. I think you're special too. You make me happy, and spending time with you is always different. I never know what to expect. I love you."

Several moments passed before I said, "I love you too." I felt like a coward, wondering if those were merely words. I was still fearful of commitment.

After that, while on other dates, Eddie would occasionally ask, "We get along great, why have two places when we can live together?"

I'd always say, "I don't know. I'm just not ready to have another long-term relationship."

Could I trust him not to leave me for someone younger and more exciting if I became boring or tiresome? Or, would I hurt him, like I was so sure I had done in the past? Several weeks later, over dinner at a nearby restaurant, he handed me airline tickets to Florida for the two of us. This was a new level and too serious.

I told him, "No, I'm sorry, I don't want to go to Florida."

After that, each time he offered me anything, I'd always say no. In, hindsight, I now know I acted like a cold, self-centered bitch.

We had been dating for about eight months when everything changed.

I was walking home from the grocery store with a plastic bag in each hand. I'd done it many times before. Only two blocks away, my chest tightened. I began to sweat. My breathing went from good to bad. I slowly made my way back home and collapsed on the couch until I felt better. I didn't go to my doctor or say anything to anyone.

Several days later, it happened again, this time walking to the DMV to renew my driver's license. I couldn't go any further. It was pouring rain, and I sat there on a bench in the park, soaking wet until I felt well enough to go home. I didn't tell Eddie what was going on. My doctor set me up with a cardiologist who ordered a stress test.

After a few minutes on the treadmill, they stopped me. I was diagnosed with heart disease and needed surgery. It was scheduled for the following week. I drove to the hospital alone and checked in. They called me back where I changed, and they placed an IV in my arm.

I was then interviewed by everyone who stopped in until I was wheeled into the Cath Lab. I have very few memories of the angiogram. After it was done, they sent me to recovery and told me they'd found three arteries on my heart with seventy to ninety percent blockages and I'd been scheduled for an angioplasty.

I didn't call Eddie.

HOW I MET MY OTHER

I knew he'd worry. I wasn't even sure how I'd cope and thought it would be better if I went through this by myself. The night before the procedure I stayed with another friend who lived close to the hospital. The next morning, my friend dropped me off. This time they gave me something lovely before surgery to calm me down. In the end, it was a success.

The next morning Eddie surprised me when he entered my room. I don't know how he knew. Stunned I said, "God, Eddie, I'm happy to see you. But you're going to make me cry like a baby!"

I'll never forget, he was wearing sneakers, a yellow tee shirt and the sexiest, shortest, cutoff jeans imaginable. My chest squeezed in a good way.

He sat in the chair beside my bed. "You should have told me. I could have been here for you. I thought you were ending it all when I found out you were in the hospital."

I'd been so wrong. "I'm sorry, I was only thinking of myself. I'm good at that."

He leaned over. "I want all this to be in the past. When you're discharged, I want all of us—you, me, and my dog—to go to my aunt's place on Harker's Island. It's just inside the Outer Banks of North Carolina. I'll help you get over this. I love you."

We did, and he did.

Eddie was like a mother hen. He entertained me, cooked for me, made sure I took my pills, and worried about me. We would lie on the floor reading the Sunday newspaper together. He didn't act like I was a burden. I was happy and safe. Eddie and I often walked his dog around Shell Point, a small beach on the island, to exercise and collect seashells. It was a fairytale that ended too soon.

I was softening. Eddie was good for me. Perhaps, it was finally time to let him into my life. Still, the old worries had their hold on me. One day, we were in the car heading to my place. I was drinking a beer, an absolute no, no. In another car, a man waggled his finger and mouthed "shouldn't do that" as he eyed my open container.

We passed under a pedestrian bridge, and I thought about the elevator and my fear of falling. I was allowing another fear—commitment—to rule me. Eddie had done nothing but shown me the depth of his character and soul in North Carolina by caring for me. I was too hard on him. "Shouldn't do that" became my new catch phrase. Why couldn't I put my fears aside? Here was a man who had shown me nothing but goodness and love.

I finally understood what I needed to do and began to laugh. Suddenly, all the things I'd carried for so many years fell away. I felt joy. At that moment I knew beyond a doubt I loved Eddie.

Better yet, I knew he truly loved me. I could finally talk honestly about our living together without squirming with fear of what might happen later.

That man in the other car will never know his admonition that day had such a profound effect on me.

We moved Eddie out of his condo and in with me, where Eddie being Eddie, soon made our house a home, something it hadn't been before. Several years later we retired and moved to Florida to be closer to his children. I love his children as if they are biologically mine. They now have their own children who call me Baba, which I've heard means father in Persian. We also reconnected with his ex-wife, her husband, and her stepchildren.

HOW I MET MY OTHER

My life is full. I have Eddie's children, their stepbrothers, wives, husbands, and cousins to love and enjoy. Together we share marriages, births, holidays, birthdays, day care celebrations, and other events as a large extended family.

I would never have had all this if it weren't for Eddie.

He and I celebrated thirty years together in July 2018 and six years of marriage that October. Neither of us will abandon the other.

My life is blessed—I love and my love is returned—and I am happy.

All I Did Was Open the Door

The Story of Melody and Myke

Year: 1971
By Melody Groves

Doors. I'd never considered the true importance of a simple door—wood or metal, screen or glass. What are doors used for? Letting in or letting out. Science fiction allows that black holes are doors to other worlds. Poets write that eyes are the door to the soul (okay, I took literary liberty here). And carpenters build doors to the future.

Turns out, my own future hinged on opening a door.

Ever since I was old enough to know boys were different from girls, I've swooned over blond, blue-eyed guys. The rest of the body needed to be pleasing, but something about blond hair and blue eyes drew me in. What it was exactly, I couldn't say. Maybe the color of their locks reminded me of sunshine. Possibly the scintillating eyes were reminiscent of bottomless oceans. Maybe, just maybe, it was because I wasn't.

On my first driver's license, my eyes were hazel. A slightly nutty, nondescript word I didn't like the sound of. On the following licenses they were green. More enticing. And my hair? Definitely not blonde. Though I started life as a platinum, by elementary school it had darkened to a mundane brown— certainly nothing to flaunt.

So, I mentally stalked almost every blond, blue-eyed fella I spotted, at least the ones within my age range and tall like my dad at a full six feet. I'd giggle when they looked my way, my stomach fluttering. And those guys on television? Oh my. I sat glued to the screen wishing, hoping, somehow they'd teleport into my house and sweep me off my feet as I ran my fingers through their golden tresses. I'd peer into their baby blues, floating in the pool of possibilities. I'd find my guy, I was sure.

As an older teenager, I was fortunate to live on a Naval base in the far Pacific during the height of the Vietnam War. Sailors poured out of every doorway and hatch of the military establishment. Tall ones, short ones, fat ones, thin ones. Officers: enlisted and in between. Hallelujah! Some of them were blond with blue eyes! One summer, I worked at the base library, where sailors came to read the latest issue of *Stars and Stripes*. Every chance I got, I carried that newspaper around the library like a candle hoping to attract Navy moths. Much to my happiness, one man, sporting the requisite hair and eye color, buzzed around my flame. Within weeks I discovered when he worked indoors, his hair soon turned brown. And, no, faux sun-bleached locks would never do.

I was tagged an opportunist by my jealous friends back in the States, and I lived up to the label. I prided myself on single-handedly supporting the morale of the 7th Fleet. While I wasn't the only girl on base, I was one of the few who was of legal dating age. Plus, my father was a civilian with officer's privileges. Though some didn't believe, it made dating me a tad easier for them. Because I was on a base filled with sailors headed for The 'Nam, I had plenty to choose from. I selected the ones I wanted and dated several. It was a strange time. The men were either on ships, so they were in port briefly, returning in a week or two, or soon headed to another duty station thousands of miles away. We all knew our relationships were temporary.

Although my dad was a civilian, we had the privilege of living in officer's housing. The sailors I knew were enlisted, which made visiting me at home awkward, if not impossible. Plus, they didn't have cars. So, my blonds and I spent afternoons at the beach, hanging out in the Officers' Club, or square dancing. Heck, I even took one to my junior-senior prom. I also checked out my fellow high school classmates. However, in my minuscule senior class (total of 28), there were only eight boys, and not one had the obligatory hues. Because no one fit my requirements, it left me stalking, er, seeking, boyfriends on base.

One who especially stands out in my memory was Australian. He was delightful, enchanting, and spoke with a heart-fluttering accent. At sixteen, I was enamored with a man who denied he kept kangaroos in his backyard. He said he'd seen them only at the zoo. I allowed him this little lie, knowing full well they hopped all over the country.

This particular blond, while about four years older than me, rocked my world more than once. At a lovely dinner one evening, he suddenly proposed. Stunned, I cited my young age, along with the fact I planned to finish high school before settling down. I didn't have experience dealing with issues like this, so I put him at arm's length until my girlfriends and I could sort it out. I mulled over his offer for a couple of weeks while his ship went to sea to participate in Australian and U.S. Naval war games. Of course, the answer would still be no, but I was interested in what else he might suggest. Upon his return, he had yet another surprise for me. He whipped out his wallet and showed me a photo of a stunning woman sitting on the beach, blowing a kiss.

"She's gorgeous! Your sister?" It certainly wasn't his mom.

"Uh . . ." He stuttered and stammered, finally gulping, "My Sheila . . . My intended. We're getting married soon as I get back," he said.

"You . . . what?" I moved in for a better look, then backed away, appalled at the insult. My heart thudded extra hard—was I relieved or sad? Both. I wasn't sure whether to kick him or cry, so I turned my back and marched off. Were all Australians two timing louts? I hoped one of those kangaroos would kick him right where it counted. I vowed to be more careful when choosing who to stalk. Eventually, he sailed off leaving me wiser for the experience.

After graduating high school, I came back home and immediately started college. Blond men attended there, too, it turned out, and their blue eyes beckoned. I dated a few, but my studies didn't allow much time for stalking. Plus, I lived at home with my parents. When my dad would go to the store, he'd always ask, "Need anything?"

My standard reply: "Six foot, blond, blue-eyed." He'd shake his head, chuckle, and step out the door. He never did bring me one.

All I Did Was Open the Door

Being a drama major meant many hours in a dark theater, not outside scouting the campus for the man of my dreams, my stalking momentarily on hold. Fortuitously, a fellow thespian who was also into screenwriting and filmmaking was putting together a Thanksgiving-themed TV show about a family's son returning from war. It was a homecoming I was all too familiar with. He asked if I would like to play the part of the young wife left home when the soldier was deployed. I jumped at the chance.

This aspiring director was in search of the right family, and he thought my parents and I were perfect for the parts. He set a date for the talent and crew to meet to go over the script. He called it "pre-production." Where better to meet than the large living room of my parents' house?

At the appointed time, the chime announced their arrival and I opened the front door, ushering in the director and four college film students who would be the "crew." We exchanged introductions as they filed in until the last one passed in front of me. I froze, the doorknob still firmly in hand. My mouth flopped open and, like in the old Tex Avery cartoon cliché, my eyes bugged out of my head. There stood my Adonis. My extremely blond, extremely blue-eyed, six-foot man of my dreams. He couldn't have been more perfect if I'd sculpted him myself. I'd ordered one like him many times, but I hadn't received precisely what I wanted until that instant. He walked into my life exactly like it was meant to be, and all I did was open the door.

Everyone sat around the living room, exchanging words, themes, and ideas. I couldn't tell what they were saying because a roaring in my ears, and my stomach firmly wedged in my throat, blocked out anything of importance. I was absolutely *In Love*.

Fortunately, since we'd be working together over the next few weeks, there would be time and opportunity to become better acquainted. The company was using the director's one-bedroom bungalow as an interior set and the tight spaces often pushed us all together intimately, which was fine by me. My Adonis hauled in light stands, electrical cables, boxes of assorted mystical contraptions, and several large lighting instruments. I was familiar with lights from the theater—but I didn't tell him.

"This is a Klieg light to make three-point lighting," Adonis said, aiming the bright light at my head. "I'll put another light there," he pointed, "and one there." Checking the shadows, he held up a hand by my face, which glowed red, I was sure. I felt the burn, in no part due to the light.

"How cool is that?" I gushed, mind devoid of reasoning, mouth running on its own.

"Well, it's easy, really," he said, those sapphire eyes radiating bravado. "Since I'm a journalism major specializing in television, film, and photography," at this point his chest puffed out just a bit, "we have to know lighting. Without light, it's hard to make a picture. It's really important."

He prattled on about some technical mumbo-jumbo, but I lasered in on his wide-shouldered stature, golden hair tucked behind his adorable ears, and his ocean-blue eyes. It turned out there was a big brain behind all that beauty—a double plus. He was someone I'd stalk until he thought he caught me.

A journalism major, huh? An emphasis in TV production, yeah? That was similar to theater, I reasoned, and the buildings were basically across the street from each other. I began hanging out at the campus television studio every chance I got and always happened to run into him. In return, he always happened to stop by the theater. We both also *happened* to enjoy photography, spending many hours together in the darkroom.

Unlike fairy tales and fantasies, however, it would take some work on my part to make a successful relationship. Apparently, I wasn't the only one who found Adonis amazingly gorgeous, intelligent, witty, and blond. Behind my back and later to my face, I discovered the college crowd referred to me as part of his harem.

I was not willing to be defined as a groupie or some sort of disciple. I mentally rolled up my sleeves and pledged: "All's fair in love and war. And this is WAR with a capital W." While I'd already admitted to being a stalker and willing to go to great lengths to get who I wanted, I wasn't about to stoop to making threats or starting nasty rumors. There would be no mudslinging here. I'd simply be my sweet conniving self, and continue to scheme.

But I didn't have to scheme. Life has a way of intervening. One afternoon, as I stood in the television studio's brand new control room, mooning over my hopefully-soon-to-be-boyfriend, a petite yet well-endowed redhead sashayed up to him. They shared a tender hug, and she whispered what I figured were sweet nothings. Off they went. Should I follow? My legs moved in that direction, but a friend blocked my way.

"Got news for you," she said, knowing how I felt about my blond.

I peered around her shoulder in time to see the outside door close, his back melting into the sunlight. Sighing, I turned my attention to her. "What kinda news?"

She cocked her head toward where my man exited with the redhead. "Simone. Party girl." She lowered her voice. "Flunked out of school. Her parents are t-ic-ked. She's leaving. Driving back home to Ohio."

Glory be and hallelujah! Ohio was a far place—two thousand miles far. Thank goodness for college parties and outraged parents. I had a chance now. Over the ensuing weeks, I elbowed two other "harem" members to the sidelines, pushing my way to the forefront and into his heart, I hoped. We spent more and more time together.

Our first official date was a doozy. Months after we'd filmed the TV show—which initially brought us together and of which I vaguely remember seeing the finished product—I invited him to share Sam Peckinpah's recent movie *The Wild Bunch*. I loved Westerns, and this was rated one of the best. A whole new type of filmmaking, they claimed.

The movie was showing on campus for free (always a good thing for college students). We sat three rows back and in the center. I wanted to be up close and personal to study the movie craft. In my theater makeup class, I'd been experimenting with and reading a great deal on the use of fake blood. No more chocolate syrup, which film, television, and theater had used for decades. No more mineral oil and vegetable coloring. Hollywood make-up artists had at last perfected blood.

Fascinated by the most recent pretend blood, which contained tiny plastic balls allowing it to coagulate like the real stuff, I *mansplained* the process, speaking so that even he could understand, before the movie started. Adonis nodded at the right parts, asked a couple of questions, but mostly listened.

"For the actors who get their necks, throats or wrists cut, make-up artists glue a thin metal strip against the actor's skin. Then they put a blood pack over that and cover it with makeup."

The topic was outside his purview of lighting, but for the sake of the first date, he feigned polite interest. "Huh," he said.

"So, when they cut somebody's throat, it squirts blood like a real cut, but nobody's hurt, see?" I went on. "Isn't that fascinating?" I had turned sideways in my seat pantomiming the slicing. "I'm gonna try doing that on Billy in class next week."

He snickered and patted my hand. "Let me know how that works out." I think he mumbled under his breath, "Hope he survives."

The lights went down, and we settled in for a romantic romp through a good ol' shoot-em-up Western. While I figured this date would neither make nor break us—probably—I hoped it would at least be a memorable evening. Within moments, blood splattered across the screen, moviegoers hid their eyes. Not me. On the edge of my seat, I kept shouting, "Great blood!"

Adonis nodded.

"Did ya see that?" I gasped with glee while others around us held hands to their lips.

My companion, sitting relaxed in his seat, pointed. "Amazing! Single source night-for-day lighting through the dirty, broken window." He glanced at me. "Who'd of thought they could do that?"

"I know! Right?" I hadn't heard what he'd said, but figured it was about the bloody effects. "What a great way to stab somebody!"

During the remaining bloodbath, I felt his gaze on me from time to time, the beginning of a grin tugging up one corner of his luscious mouth.

"Neato!" I shouted again. "Did ya see that? He sliced his throat! All the way across—"

The woman sitting in front of us abruptly stood, whipped around, scowled, and pointed a manicured finger at me. "You're sick!" She and her four friends huffed off. Other people around us got up and moved farther away. Mutterings abounded.

I paid no attention. I was busy reveling in marvelous film makeup. My date chuckled, but I figured, being a media major, he was reacting to the outstanding cinematography and breathtaking effects. The credits rolled and then the lights came on. I squealed, clapped, came back to reality, and scanned the room. We were pretty much alone, except for one couple way in the back busy making out.

"That was awesome!" I raved to Adonis. "Who knew there'd be so much blood?" I rattled on and on, deliberating the merits of gunshot wounds versus knife slices, each needing various blood packs.

He slid an arm around my shoulders, effectively ending my babbling. The weight of his arm sent shivers of pleasure over my body. He squeezed tight then let go.

We walked out into a warm evening. Our first date would be over momentarily, and I hoped there would be more. The movie had been delightful. The moonrise brilliant. He—breathtaking. Hand in hand we strolled to the parking lot. Soon, he'd head back to his dorm and me to my home, three miles away.

Leaning against my car, he drew me in and gave me a peck on the cheek. "You know," he whispered. "I knew you were different the first time I met you."

I wasn't sure if it was a compliment or not, so I waited for the other shoe to drop. For once, I remained quiet, except for the earthquake in my stomach.

He held me at arms' length, his denim-blue eyes traveling over my face. "Anybody crazy as you has got to be fun!"

I assumed that was a good thing. I reached for the car door, and he placed his hand on mine, his soft skin making me smile. He moved in close. "Let's open this door together and see where it leads us."

Why not? He had me at "door."

Get an update on Melody and Adonis (a.k.a. Myke) and see pictures at www.orangeblossombooks.com

How Timely It Was

Out of the Park

The Story of Tim and Arielle
Year: 2002, 2006
By Tim and Arielle Haughee

2002: Tim

This date didn't go as planned. Her demeanor was flat, the conversation forced and lethargic. I pulled into Arielle's apartment complex to drop her off and made a last-ditch effort to coax a smile from her. Where was the fun girl from two years ago?

I had been hopeful for this night as our date approached. I was a sophomore in college at the University of Florida and enjoyed making friends and meeting girls as an independent young man. I met Arielle several years prior at a summer job back home in Orlando and remembered her to be quite attractive, with a spirited sense of humor to boot.

At nineteen years old, I wasn't necessarily ready to settle down for a long-term relationship. I had several fairly lengthy ones in high school, always playing the role of the serious boyfriend. But as a college student, I wasn't particularly interested in being a significant other. Rather, my goal was quite selfish: I wanted to only worry about myself. In the romantic world, this translated into trying to meet as many cute girls as possible.

I wanted to see if my sweet-talking ways would have any success on Arielle—maybe there was still time. I leaned over on the console and flashed my best smile. "I had fun tonight. I'm glad we got a chance to do this. We were always dating other people when we worked together. It's the first time we've both been single."

She released a nervous laugh. Laughter was good, that meant I was heading in the right direction. I leaned a little closer. "You look really pretty tonight."

Her eyes widened.

The sound of the door handle jolted me out of my thoughts of a kiss.

"Thanks for taking me out!" Arielle hopped out of the car faster than a squirrel in traffic.

A swing and a miss.

"No problem," I said, trying to regain my pride. I paused, figuring out what to say next. Definitely not *let's do this again sometime.* "Have a nice night."

She waved and walked a little quicker than was polite up to her door. Jeez. I wasn't that bad. I pulled out of Arielle's complex and tried to figure out what went wrong. We always seemed to have a good rapport. Shouldn't this night have been a breeze? Why did it seem like there wasn't even the remotest bit of a connection between us? My plan for the night was to take her out for a movie and ice cream and see where things went from there.

On our way to the movie theater, we updated each other on our co-workers from our previous summer job. It was a pretty tame subject, delivered in straight, informative tones. It was clear this girl was not the same vibrant, energetic one I remembered.

Unfortunately, my plan for seeing a movie backfired. When conversation is flat on a date, seeing a movie together only seems to exacerbate the distance. Two hours of looking straight ahead, with effectively no verbal exchanges between us. Awkward, to say the least.

By the time the movie ended, we weren't sure where to take our conversation.

Instead, we proceeded with our plan to walk across the shopping center to the ice cream shop and grab a few scoops. We sat on the steps outside and ate, not saying much of anything. A meth lab had more chemistry than we did. I couldn't pinpoint one part where things went completely south. The whole thing had been one soggy interaction after another, quite a disappointment.

I waited at a red light and reminded myself the date didn't matter much anyway. I'd already contented myself with being single for at least the next few semesters. I'd go out with other girls, and one thing was for sure, I wouldn't be going out with this girl again.

Arielle

I stepped inside and locked my front door, leaning my head back on the dingy white metal. Did he want to kiss me? I panicked and leaped out of the car. I waited years to go out with *the* Tim, and nothing happened. No connection, no spark, no sizzle. It was like drinking a glass of room temperature water. And I don't just kiss any guy, especially one I find to be so...ordinary. Even though Tim was incredibly cute and he used to make me laugh, something was off about tonight. I could sense he wasn't really into the relationship thing and I didn't want to risk it with a party boy, especially one that could put me to sleep with his conversation.

I knew what that meant.

Sighing, I headed for the phone in my room. My boyfriend and I decided to take a break and see if we wanted to date other people. If Tim, the one I'd always wanted a chance with didn't work out, I only had one alternative if I didn't want to be alone.

Pictures of Paul peeked out from almost every corner of my simple room—a quilted cover on my bed, a small desk, and a few books. Even though I was eighteen and supposed to be having the time of my life finally outside the house, I spent most of my time going to class or hanging out with Paul. I hadn't made many friends in my new college town or figured out what I wanted to do with my life yet. I picked up the closest frame and examined the handsome face and brown eyes.

He wasn't the nicest to me.

Paul refused to drive up to Gainesville, always insisting I come down to Orlando instead. I would often make the trip down several times a week. He also told me things like, "I'm not interested in hearing about your school so don't talk about it," and "You're the only one who wants to marry their high school boyfriend." But he was cute and smart, and I really cared about him. No one was perfect, and I had no idea who I would be if I were alone. I wasn't ready to find out.

This date with Tim didn't work so I would put all my energy into my previous boyfriend. I would be exactly what Paul wanted—calm, quiet, and giving. Even though I tried before, I probably wasn't trying hard enough.

I hit speed dial and went back into the comfort of my familiar relationship.

Tim

I dimmed my headlights before pulling into the driveway, hoping my college buddies-turned-roommates didn't notice my obvious early arrival. Unless I was willing to sneak in through a window (I wasn't), there was only one way into this 1950s, ranch-style rental house awkwardly tucked in a small neighborhood between the University's "official" hotel and a Save-a-Lot grocery store. I slowly turned the front door handle and gave a slight push, but the old brass hardware of the doorframe betrayed my attempted inconspicuousness.

"Boy, that was fast," exclaimed a voice from the living room. "How'd it go?"

My buddy, Stoney (only his family calls him Mike), was never one for beating around the bush, especially when he'd been working on the back half of a case of Coors Light.

"Is she here with you? I want to meet her. Bring 'er in," he said as he approached from around the corner.

He peered over my head and out the door with his six-foot-two-inch frame, expecting to see the cute girl I told him about earlier that day.

"Dude, where's the chick? You didn't scare her off, did ya?"

Oy.

A familiar pitter-patter raced in my direction from down the hallway. Finally, a girl who'd give me a kiss without any hesitation or prejudgment. I knelt down and happily accepted some love from Athena, our three-year-old American bulldog. She was followed by Dave, her technical owner, although we all claimed to have at least some joint ownership rights.

"Hey, buddy. Back so soon?"

Dave was the subtle one.

"Yeah," I said with a shrug. "You win some, you lose some I guess. Tonight just wasn't my night, fellas."

"Dang, dude," Stoney said. "Well, don't worry about it. Come on in and grab an ice cold beer."

Stoney always had a way of cheering people up.

"I didn't hear the story," Dave said. He followed us into the kitchen with Athena in tow. "How'd you know this girl again?"

2000: Tim

I had just arrived and clocked-in for my afternoon shift as a guest services representative at Wet 'N Wild, the water park located in the heart of Orlando's tourist district. The park was a popular employer for local high school students who wanted an easy job in a fun environment. My senior year was coming up, so

I returned to Wet 'N Wild for another summer, hopeful my earnings would assist me in buying the Mitsubishi Eclipse I recently set my eyes on.

My fellow co-worker, Anthony, seemed particularly giddy today as I entered the small guest services office located just past the ticket booths.

"Dude, have you met the new chick yet? She's pretty cute. Spunky too. Just finished up her training."

The twinkle in his eye affirmed his interest. Of course, his excitement got my antennae up too.

"Is she still here? And what's her name?"

"She's out in ticket booth three," Anthony replied. "Her name is Arielle. But don't get any ideas, I saw her first!"

"Slow down there, buddy," I retorted. "No one's claiming your territory just yet."

Despite my quasi-assurance to Anthony, I was intrigued at meeting this fresh, and apparently cute, new face.

After getting set up and logging in, I realized I should figure out an excuse to visit ticket booth three. Looking around the office, I noticed the box of new admission tickets sitting on the counter. A sly little grin overtook my face.

Better see if booth three is low on tickets, I thought.

I grabbed a stack and headed out of the office.

"Hey, where ya headed?" I heard Anthony say as the door shut behind me.

HOW I MET MY OTHER
Arielle

I leaned on the counter in the tiny ticket booth, scanning the pages of a paperback. Even though this place was the size of a closet, I felt comfortable, cozy even. A little space all to myself. My favorite part of the afternoon shift was the easy pace, about one customer every half hour. Hence the book. I drifted into the world of *Pride and Prejudice* when a tentative knock interrupted Elizabeth Bennet's musings.

I opened the locked door only to see a giant stack of tickets being held by someone in the same uniform. They lowered to reveal beautiful green eyes, then long sideburns, then a gorgeous mouth. My heart fluttered.

He smiled revealing perfect twin dimples.

All rational thought left—what I was doing, where I was, my name—all gone.

The only presence in my mind was this perfect face sent down from the heavens.

It took me a moment to realize he was speaking. I shook my head and this time heard when he mentioned something about tickets.

"Oh, yes, sure," I responded in all my brilliance.

He stepped in and sat the giant stack next to the full ticket dispenser. I'd never had anyone hand-deliver tickets to my booth. It was my responsibility to take care of the supplies.

"I'm Tim," he said. He leaned against the counter across from me, only a few feet between us. "I work in Guest Services."

Now he's hanging out? I know exactly what's going on here.

Emboldened by my knowledge of his check-out-the-new-girl plan, I pointed to the full ticket dispenser. "Good thing you brought me those extra tickets."

He laughed. "Hey, a caravan of tourist buses could descend any minute. Then you'd be overrun with—"

"Martians. Millions of them. All here with their six arms poking out of their bathing suits."

"Exactly. Ready to blast you with their ray guns if you didn't have enough tickets. So you're welcome."

We both laughed. When I looked in his warm green eyes, I was happy I found someone so easy to talk to and as incredibly cute as Tim. A niggling thought itched at the back of my head. The word *boyfriend* drifted to the front of my mind.

Crap. I had a boyfriend.

I suppressed my fascination and put on a polite smile, telling him I should get back to work. As much as this guy struck me, I was a faithful girlfriend. Maybe something could happen in the future. At least I sure hoped it did.

2006: Arielle

A green, slimy, goblin face stared at me from the shelf. Next to it sat a pumpkin with a cat cutout.

"Check this out," my friend Katie said. She reached on the side of the goblin and pressed down. Green goo slid down its cheeks under a clear layer of plastic.

"Awesome," I laughed. "But not quite what I'm looking for." It was still a few weeks before Halloween, but I couldn't help escaping the stress of my grad school class schedule to immerse myself in my favorite holiday. Though I kept busy, I felt deeply satisfied with my choice of becoming a special education teacher. I knew it was a perfect fit for me and exactly what I wanted.

"Let me guess," she said and walked over to the skimpy costumes. "You're looking for something like this?" She held up a scrap of fabric intended to be a nurse's outfit.

It was tiny. It was sleazy. It was almost perfect.

"Close."

She laughed. "Yessss! You need to be going out with more guys, and this will definitely reel a few in."

I smiled at my sweet friend. She'd been encouraging me to try dating again. After a major heartbreak from my long-distance boyfriend, then a toxic relationship with the next, I was done being quiet, complacent, and everything I thought men wanted. I was determined to be exactly what I wanted to be: me. I would make jokes, be bold, and laugh often. But was there a guy out there who would like that?

Only one way to know.

I spotted a black and white number on another rack. "This one!"

Katie eyed the striped, tight mini dress. "What's it supposed to be?"

"Jailbait."

"Perfect. Now I need a good one." She pulled a head-to-toe Chewbacca suit off the rack and draped it over her body, lifting a questioning brow.

"Where's your costume?"

"Har. You go check out while I put this back. I'm starving."

After a few more laughs and a satisfying lunch, we made our way back to my sunny yellow apartment. I hung the jailbait costume in the closet and smiled as I wondered what fun it would bring. First, I needed a new prospect, and I had a good idea where to start.

"Help me find a date," I told Katie. We sat on the couch, and I opened my laptop.

This new website "Facebook" was supposedly a great place to meet new people and connect with old friends. It was only for college students unlike MySpace, so I felt safe to explore there. I hadn't been on Facebook much but I scrolled through, and a dimpled face immediately caught my attention.

"No. Way."

"Who's that?"

"It's Tim, *the* Tim. That super cute guy I worked with back in high school."

I clicked on his picture. There he was, still as gorgeous as ever.

"Didn't you guys have that lame date?" Katie asked.

"Yes..." My eyes wandered back to that face. He had a mischievous sparkle in his eye and a little snarky smirk. Then I did what any single girl would do, I stalked through his information. "He still lives in Gainesville...is in law school...plays guitar..."

"So? You went out with him already and it was a bust."

"I wasn't fully myself the first time we went out. I was still stuck on Paul. We used to have fun when we worked together, joked around a lot. There's something there, and it just needs a second chance. I'm going to say hi."

"You can't say hi for no reason. It'll be weird. You haven't talked to him in years."

"Look!" I practically shouted. "It's his birthday in a few days. I'm going to tell him happy birthday. There. Now I have a reason."

Before Katie could stop me, I sent a quick message then closed my laptop. "There."

"You sent it?"

I responded with a smile, and she shook her head, laughing.

I promised myself I was going to be bold. What if Tim didn't like that? All I could do was wait and see.

Tim

A cool breeze blew across the courtyard as I begrudgingly made my way to the law library. It was mid-October, almost my birthday, and the months of constant heat and humidity were finally coming to an end. I was halfway through my first semester of law school—the semester that sets you apart from your peers, the one that matters most—and woefully behind.

I had only been back in Gainesville since early August. Just three weeks before that, I met a girl at the apartment complex where I was living in Orlando and jumped right into a fairly serious relationship. We were so sure everything was "meant to be," we hardly considered the challenge of long distance. Nearly six weeks after my move to Gainesville, the strain on the nascent relationship was too much. We called it quits. I'd had plenty of time chasing girls and going on dates. I was ready to get serious with someone. I thought this girl wanted it, too.

Nevertheless, I looked on the bright side. While disappointed the relationship fizzled, the constant trips back and forth to Orlando during the weekends put me squarely behind the eight ball. Final exams would be here soon enough, and my classmates were already spending most of their weekends studying. If I was going to make this law school gamble work, I needed to buckle down, and fast. Maybe this newfangled independence was just what I needed to reset my focus.

I found an empty table in the law library's main study room, which, with its gilded accents and light wood paneling, failed to match the rest of the law school's dull, unfinished concrete look that served as the hallmark of brutalist architecture. I opened up my school-issued laptop and launched my study outline for *Constitutional Law*.

Before opening up the associated textbook, I decided to log onto Facebook and see what my friends were up to.

An indicator showed I had a new message.

Very interesting, I thought. Arielle Barritt. Hadn't heard from her in years. I certainly wasn't expecting a message from her.

I clicked on the screen to open it:

Hey there! I saw from your profile page that you're back up in Gainesville. Me too! Doing my master's in teaching at UF. Anyway, saw your birthday was coming up - happy birthday!

HOW I MET MY OTHER

I almost did a double take. That was out of the blue.

While her message did get my attention, I immediately reminded myself of our date years prior, which went over like a fart in church. I shook my head.

A quick response should do the trick:

Hello there to you! Yes, I'm recently back in town. Just started law school this semester. It's a bit different, but I'm getting used to it. Glad to know that you're up here too. Thanks for the b-day wishes. We'll have to get together sometime.

That last sentence was a throwaway. While I appreciated her message, I struck out on the first date and was scared away for good. I couldn't imagine going through that disappointment again.

I hit "send" and closed my laptop.

I procrastinated enough. Time to open up my textbook and read some boring precedential case law from a bygone era. Another exciting weekend.

A couple weeks later, with football season in full swing, I came out into the living room with my laptop to join the guys in watching some early afternoon football games while I updated my study outline. I'd been in my room for hours and needed a change of scenery. I could use a little more fun in my life.

"Sack him! Sack him! Take him down!!"

Stoney and Dave high-fived as the quarterback was viciously driven to the ground.

Focusing may be a little harder than I thought.

"Tim, you ready for a brewski?" Dave asked. "Got a new case in the fridge if you want one."

"Not quite yet," I replied. "Almost done. Twenty minutes and I should be good."

"Oh, that's not a holding penalty!" Stoney yelled at the TV. "Come on refs, get it together!"

I re-read the same line in my outline several times but still couldn't focus. Ugh. Officially distracted, I opened up Facebook to see what was the latest.

Another new message from Arielle:

Hey! So...when you taking me out? I believe you said we should get together, sir.

Well, well, well.

She certainly had my attention now. This version of Arielle seemed different, more like the old one from our work days at Wet 'N Wild. Plus, she still looked pretty dang good.

She set the line, so I decided to bite:

Well, hello! You are certainly right. Where are my manners, making a sweet girl wait so long on me? I agree, we should go out. You just tell me when.

I kept the laptop on while I cracked open my first beer and watched the game with the fellas. Athena jumped up on the couch and curled up next to me.

A few minutes later, I received her reply:

How about tonight? There's a Halloween party in my complex. My friends and I are going. You should come too!

I didn't expect we'd get together the same day. Unfortunately, I already made plans, but I wanted keep things moving in a positive direction:

Shoot! That sounds tempting, but I can't do tonight. We're getting ready to make the trek up to Jacksonville in a few hours for the Gator football game against Georgia. I'm gonna have to miss out. However, next weekend is wide open. What do you think? You pick the time, and I'll handle the rest.

Arielle

Red v-neck dress? Backless black top? Denim micro-mini? Ugh. All my outfit choices either said desperate or slutty. And I was neither. I wanted to exude *fun* because that is what I was all about. I glanced at the little black and white striped number hanging in the back and sighed. A missed opportunity. We never did go out on Halloween after Katie got the stomach bug. I settled on a form-fitting gray scoop neck and jeans. It would show off just enough while not being too much.

We arranged to go out on a Friday in early November. Dinner and an improv comedy show. This time I wouldn't force myself to tone down or be quiet. I would be completely me and enjoy my time, however it unfolded.

It had been years since I'd seen Tim. People didn't change that much in four years, or did they? He could have turned into someone who only talks about themselves. Or doesn't hold open doors. Or says "Ar-kan-sass." Or eats burritos sideways, biting in the middle. I grabbed my phone.

"Katie! I can't do this!"

"What are you talking about?"

"Tim. He eats burritos sideways."

"What? Is he with you now? Are you guys eating Mexican?"

"No he's not here yet...I just...have a feeling."

Silence. It probably only lasted a few seconds, but it felt like a lifetime. She sighed. "Okay. I think you're really feeling a bit anxious because you had a crappy date years ago and you have no idea who this person is today. Theoretically, he could be worse, right?"

I stopped pacing. "Maybe."

"Relax. You're getting worked up over nothing. Just go out and have fun and if he sucks, call me, and I'll come get you."

I looked down at my gray shirt and jeans. Fun, I reminded myself. It didn't matter what happened in the past or how much I'd been hurt because tonight was just tonight. I thanked Katie and hung up, promising to call her right after.

The door buzzer went off.

I headed for the stairs, took a deep breath and told myself no matter what waited for me, I got to choose how the night went.

Dimples. That was all my eyes focused on as I approached the gate. My face lit into a smile, and I opened the door. Tim looked exactly the same, gorgeous green eyes, beautiful smile, and most likely knew how to eat Mexican food. Butterflies flitted through my stomach. Nothing would hold me back from enjoying my time with the guy I always wanted to date—no personal insecurities, other relationships, or feelings that something was "off." This was finally my chance with *the* Tim.

A wave of energy swelled through me.

"Hey, Tim," I said and gave him a quick hug.

"Hey yourself." Those dimples got impossibly bigger. He walked me to his car and opened the door. I popped in and could barely contain my ocean of excitement.

I have no idea what words came out of my mouth as he drove but I chatted on...and on...and he smiled and laughed, happily conversing. There was an instant ease that was missing last time, like talking to a best friend.

"You hungry?" he asked when we sat down at our table on the patio of the little bistro. Twinkle lights hung above us and cars zipped past on the street nearby.

"I could eat." I'd made the mistake years ago of eating barely anything the day of a date and clearing my plate that evening, horrifying the guy with my monstrous appetite. Not tonight. "I'll have the portobello sandwich," I told the waitress.

"It's our wine tasting night. Which flight would you like to try?"

"Wine tasting?" We both said, then laughed.

Tim picked the red and I settled on the white. We talked about school and our families while we waited, each enjoying the first of three glasses of wine. My sandwich arrived, and the mushroom slid all over the bun, seeping sauce everywhere. No way I could keep eating this disaster. More would end up on my clothes than in my stomach.

The next glass of wine arrived.

"How are you liking the mahi?" I asked.

"Mahi? I ordered the dolphin sandwich."

I laughed. "Dolphin is mahi. It's just a nickname they use. You aren't eating real dolphin."

He snorted. "I know that. But it's not mahi."

"Well, what is it then? It's totally mahi."

We each reached for our phones, determined to get fish expert, phone-a-friend proof. His friend swore it was dolphin fish while mine informed me it was in fact mahi. Of course, I was right.

We playfully argued about it all the way to the improv show. I stumbled a bit getting out of the car. That third glass of wine on a very light dinner was not doing me any favors. Luckily, this show was on campus, and we wouldn't be able to order any more drinks. Plenty of time for me to sober up. Tim held out his arm. I couldn't tell if it was gentlemanly courtesy or because he saw me almost trip over the flat floor, but I didn't care. I took it.

This show was my idea, and Tim seemed excited I showed interest in comedy. He held open the wide, wooden door to the campus "pub," and my spirits fell the instant I scanned the crowd.

Freshmen.

Tables full of geeky eighteen-year-olds straight from their dorms. *Way to pick the entertainment, Arielle.* I couldn't let this little hiccup ruin everything. There was only one thing to do.

Tim

I'd been to many comedy clubs in the past, including some of the hip, famous ones like The Improv and The Comedy Store located in the heart of the Sunset Strip in Los Angeles. This was not one of those clubs.

I slowly turned my head to look over at Arielle, who planned this part of our outing. Her eyes met mine with a hint of mischief.

"Let's go over there." She nudged me toward an empty balcony area. It didn't hurt that she looked stunning.

The lights dimmed, and the host walked on stage, introducing the show with a terrible Harvey Dangerfield impression. She leaned over, which I certainly appreciated, and whispered, "Table three, red shirt."

My eyes fell on a taller kid with messy dark hair and long arms. What was I supposed to see?

"Plays backgammon in a hula skirt every Wednesday or eats live cockroaches?" she said.

I felt a smirk grow on my face. "He's got that long torso, great for hula dancing."

She laughed. "Agree. Table seven, green and yellow hat."

A new person came on stage, but my attention was in the crowd. The hat belonged to a guy with greasy long blond hair and a stained t-shirt.

"Makes sculptures with his toenail clippings or can play the mandolin with his nose."

"He looks like a hidden talent type of guy. I'm going with the mandolin."

We kept up the game, making our own little comedy show together. Something was definitely different this time. My first hint was when I picked her up, she seemed so happy to be in the car with me. Then during our little debate about the dolphin sandwich—which I won—I got a glimpse of the old spunky girl from when we first met. Come to think of it, there hadn't been a dull moment yet. I hadn't laughed this much in a long time.

About forty-five minutes into the show, we decided we were ready to get back out on the town. While we both got a little tipsy during dinner, our respective alcohol buzzes had worn off. We both agreed that a few more drinks were in order.

"So, where should we go next?" I asked when we were outside.

"How about some dancing?" Arielle had that look of mischief in her eyes again.

I couldn't say no.

Luckily, we were only a few blocks away from Market Street, the place to go for dancing. The temperature felt like it had dropped another ten degrees since dinner. Arielle shivered as we crossed the street: The perfect excuse. I put my arms around her and rubbed her shoulders.

"You think you're gonna be able to make it?"

She laughed, and I loved the sound.

We arrived at Market Street, which was already firing on all cylinders even though it was a few hours before last call. After making our way to the bar and snagging a few drinks, Arielle grabbed my hand.

HOW I MET MY OTHER

"Time to dance!" she yelled over the pulsating music.

It was a good thing I had a few drinks in me and was loosened up. Had I been sober, the date would have come to a crashing halt after she saw my dance moves.

On the dance floor, it was clear that Arielle had no trouble busting a move. No wonder she wanted to show off her skills. I just tried my best to keep up. The jokes and conversation kept on even as we moved.

The more time I spent with her, the more I realized she really was a great girl. Funny and energetic. Sweet and caring. Intelligent and sarcastic. I liked being with her, and she seemed to enjoy my company too. Maybe this one could be for keeps.

After a few more songs, I needed a little break from pretending to be a decent dancer.

I stepped to the side of the dance floor, and Arielle followed. Though we hadn't really had a pause in conversation all night, one had just developed.

Arielle looked up at me with her beautiful brown eyes.

"So, what do you want to do now?"

I knew the answer.

"What do I want to do?"

I leaned down and pressed my lips to hers.

Arielle

The kiss was soft and sweet. Definitely not what I was expecting after dancing the way I did. Maybe he was as sweet as his kiss? We had fun, my main goal for the evening, but could this be something even more? I didn't have a good track record with picking guys, and I wasn't sure how to tell if Tim was a good one.

The DJ announced last call and he took my hand, guiding me toward the door. This date we'd had an instant, easy connection. We talked, we laughed, we kissed, and everything was perfect. What was so different about us this time? Could it be me?

My head spun more than the disco lights hanging from the ceiling. Maybe it was the alcohol. I needed to clear my head so I could think. I soon realized the only solution.

"Taco Bell!"

Tim laughed. "What?"

"Let's get Taco Bell. It's 2 AM. They're open until four."

We walked down the empty street, hand-in-hand.

"After you, my lady." He bowed and held open the door to our salvation.

We grabbed a sackful of goodies and headed back toward my apartment where we could turn on a lame sitcom and make fun of it while scarfing down some nachos. The food gave me a bit more level-headedness, and as I looked at Tim, I realized it couldn't just be me. Both of us were different this time.

The laughs, the fun, the easiness continued until our heads nodded down as we sat on the couch. He stretched out and pulled me alongside him, both of us still wearing our shoes. I eased into a comfortable sleep even though we were crushed together on my small, beat up couch.

Sometime in the night, I was awakened by a soft kiss pressed on the top of my head.

He was completely passed out and revealed who he truly was, not just a fun party-boy, but a sweet, loving guy who I connected with. I'd been myself, nothing held back, and he enjoyed it and wanted to be around me. I snuggled in closer, knowing that this time it was for real.

Tim

Our first date was a strike out, but luckily we were able to get back up to bat.

Many elements have to be just right for a baseball player to make that perfect hit. He needs to be the correct distance from the plate with a good stance. He has to hold the bat with his hands in the right place and at the correct angle. He must nail the exact motion of the swing. But most importantly, he needs to time everything exactly right.

Lots of pieces had to fall into place before Arielle and I could be together. We both needed to be in the right mindset and ready for the other person. During our "second first date," everything lined up, stance, swing, and of course, timing. We were ready, and this time, we hit it out of the park.

Learn more about Tim and Arielle and see pictures at www.orangeblossombooks.com

Reacquainting

The Story of KJ and Greg
Year: 2006
By Greg Hill

As a pragmatist, I never considered that my first meeting with my ideal partner would involve me, glassy-eyed and admiring his presence, dumbstruck in a moment surrounded by sparks and fireworks. But he did appear at the right time to save me from trouble and earn my honest gratitude. It was on the Fourth of July, so I guess it just turned out that way.

During the summer of 2000, students finishing sophomore spring term were required to be on campus and take a normal load of classes. It was a feature of Dartmouth, our college. The summer was beautiful in New Hampshire, and every summer the sophomore class got to feel the pride of being the only—and therefore the oldest—class on the campus.

For the Fourth of July, my sorority hosted their fraternity for a mixed doubles pong tournament—a thinly guised excuse for close contact and perhaps a softening of inhibitions. As the sorority's president for the summer term, I was supposed to be one of several partygoers committed to being sober for the evening. The night wore on, and losing teams slowly disappeared from the basement where the games were played. Winning teams progressed in the single elimination tournament.

The social chairs had paired me with Brandon, my ex-boyfriend from freshman year. His fraternity assigned him the title of Risk Manager for the summer term, meaning he was also sober and charged with helping to make sure nothing got too out of hand. So, we played with water instead of beer. We lost our pong game early and spent the rest of the night casually chatting. Discussing details of the tournament, like who was playing well, fortunately prevented my having to hear him explain the nuances of risk management or how, being from the east coast, I could never fully appreciate the importance of football to the social and political hierarchies in his home state, Kansas.

I had broken up with Brandon over a year ago. I considered the breakup amicable. He was courteous and doting, but not quite intellectually stimulating, a shortcoming I overlooked because he was on the football team and fairly strong, characteristics I am ashamed now to admit then clouded my judgment regarding our compatibility. He, however, always considered our breakup temporary. His parents met in college just like we had, they overcame a brief breakup, and he was confident he was following their proven blueprint for a successful, long-term, football-enthusiastic, life together.

Late in the evening, as the pong games began to wind down, I returned to my room. Though I was an elected officer in the sorority, whenever there was a party, and everyone around me seemed to be having a great time—and especially in times like that summer when I didn't have a boyfriend—I felt almost like an outsider. In a moment of weakness I wished I could have blamed on alcohol, I invited Brandon back to my room, an offer he did not decline.

At about three o'clock in the morning, we were startled awake, and I came to my senses in increasing layers of panic. *What the—?...What's happening?...Where is?...Who's making that noise?* At first, the fire alarm's shrieking pulses jerked my body up before I could process what was going on. Next, I caught up to reality and started worrying if there was a real fire and if everyone was safe. Various voices from upstairs shouted through the blaring alarm:

"Kara set off the alarm! It's not a real fire."

"Kara and Kevin set off firecrackers in the bathroom!"

"No, it was in the hallway!"

"Hey, looks like some of the guys, uh, slept over."

At least there was no fire, and no one was in any danger. Still, our sorority has a national charter that specifically prohibits men from spending the night. I won't say this was anywhere near the first time this specific bylaw had been violated. It was simply a matter of getting Kevin and Brandon, and any other guys who might still be inside, out of the house and off the property. I was confident this would not be difficult.

Unfortunately, that wasn't the only problem.

The fire alarm meant security officers from the college already would have been notified and would be speeding toward our sorority house. That realization pushed me to the next layer of panic. The same security officers were also responsible for monitoring fraternity and sorority parties to make sure all kegs were officially registered. We hadn't registered for this party, and

I was sure no one had cleaned up any of the beer that was certain to be left sitting out in the open. I ran to the basement, and my heart sank at what I already knew to be true. Hundreds of plastic cups, many half-filled with cheap beer, littered every horizontal surface. Multiple kegs, some empty, some full and heavy, stood around the perimeter.

How could I get thirty sleepy and drunk or hung-over women to help me? I could see the futility, and I foresaw immediately how the night was about to unfold: security officers would show up, angry the fire alarm had been set off. As president, I would be responsible for ushering the officers into the house and, inevitably, into the basement where our infractions would be discovered. I would be put on probation at the college, and our sorority would lose our charter. I would bear the blame for all of it.

I ran back upstairs. "Please," I pleaded to every sleepy face standing bewildered in the hall. "Can you please help me clean up the cups? Can you help me put away the beer? So we don't get fined? So we don't lose our house?"

"Hey, s-s-sorry!" came a slurring, laughing, voice from the far end of the hall. *Kara.*

"Just help me, please!" I yelled back, as forcefully but as nicely as I could, still fighting the din of the alarms.

One by one, they had been getting dressed and shuffling into the hallway, but no one seemed quite sure where to go. What took me a few moments to realize was that the hallway seemed twice as crowded as it should have been. Someone turned on the hall light, and all became clear: just about every woman in the hall was dragging a sloppily dressed guy behind her.

I had never been so happy to see so many violations of the no-men-overnight rule. It was like my chances to avoid disaster had, ironically, just doubled. I rushed into action, pleaded with this now double-sized army to help clean up.

"Please," I begged again, this time to a more alert audience, "Safety and Security are coming! We only have a few minutes. The basement's a mess!"

"We're on it," someone said, and everyone started dividing up the work. Hands went up, and bodies moved toward the stairwells.

"We'll work on the entryway."

"Can you guys help with the trash bins?"

"Are there gloves in the closet?"

"I can help in the basement."

Women, feeling sheepish or embarrassed, hurried around to dump plastic cups into trash barrels. Men—whether they felt sheepish too, or guilty, or just wanted to help because of their insatiable machismo—rushed to help too. With impressive speed, the downstairs and the basement were cleaned and all the people inside the house—most importantly for me, the male guests—were escorted outside. The men hurried home to escape being found by the security officers.

My heart still raced from the initial shock of the fire alarm and the subsequent panic, but my mind started to relax. At least we'd cleaned the house of the men, the beer cups and—

"The kegs!"

No one had gotten rid of them. A full keg weighs over 150

pounds. Everyone was already gathering around outside. There wouldn't be enough time to go back in and get them.

I was doomed again.

Just as I resigned myself to the worst, the back door flung open. Brandon and another guy shuffled out onto the patio, carrying the full kegs. They heaved them over their heads and into the empty dumpster by the driveway, ran back in and did the same with the empty kegs. As they lowered the fifth keg into the dumpster, the lights from the security van pulled around the corner at the end of the street.

I hurried over to the dumpster at the back of the lot. "Oh my God, thank you. Thank you!" I said to both of them. "You're saving my life here. I would be in huge trouble if those kegs stayed in the house."

Brandon pointed a thumb over to his accomplice hiding behind the dumpster. "Greg and I are more than happy to help."

Greg. He wasn't tall like Brandon, and I got the impression a keg was probably pretty heavy for him. He wasn't smiling, exactly, but something in his eyes belied the seriousness of his façade.

"Thank you, Greg." Unsure what else to do, I reached out my hand. "I'm KJ."

He laughed and took my hand. "I know," he said. The security van pulled onto the gravel driveway.

"Okay, we'd better go," Brandon said, now in a whisper.

"No, really. Thank you," I insisted, maybe more than I needed to. "I would have gotten in so much trouble if it weren't for you." Greg squinted and smiled meekly, then the two of them walked away from the house and the security van, and into the darkness.

Reacquainting

In November of 2006, I flew down to Washington, D.C. to visit my best friend from college. Jim and I met freshman year when our rooms were in the same dormitory hall. By coincidence, he and Brandon later joined the same fraternity and became roommates for their senior year.

Jim wasn't in the military but worked for a contractor that worked closely with the military, and they were going to send him to help with the war in Iraq. His work had something to do with either armor or radar, but he talked about it obscurely, like he was the only person in the world who could do whatever highly specialized job it was he claimed to do, and he pretended like talking about it would somehow mean leaking highly classified information to the enemy. I didn't know exactly why he was going, just that he was. And he didn't know exactly when they were supposed to send him, but his departure was imminent. I was visiting to see him off.

As a then second-year medical student at Dartmouth, I had no life—no free time, not even much chance to talk to friends like Jim who lived so far away. I had little sympathy for people—in business school, for example—who complained about the possibility of having to meet with their study groups on a Saturday. My weekends blurred together with my weekdays.

My life was simply four things: studying, attending class, eating, and sleeping, usually in that order, in decreasing amounts. Only because it was a scheduled weekend break between terms was it even possible to make such a trip so far away.

I had decided almost a year before, after years of trying too hard to turn available guys—Brandon and a small parade of doomed mismatches—into suitable boyfriends, that med school was not the time to meet a potential mate. Living in rural New Hampshire also didn't help. The truth is, I didn't have time for such extracurricular pursuits anyway. *Good things happen when you least expect it.* My mother kept telling me versions of that maxim, and at 26 years old, I finally gave in and accepted being single for the long-term. I hoped Mom's relationship advice would be useful someday. Maybe after medical school.

During my trip to D.C., I reconnected with some of Jim's college friends who were also living in the area. I'd known them all, tangentially at least, through Jim, but I had almost always had a boyfriend and probably because of that I never really knew too much about any of Jim's friends.

One of them was Greg, a high school teacher who had been living in the D.C. area for a couple years, but whom I hadn't seen since college. He had the same gentle eyes and subtle smile I remembered from that near-disaster in my sorority six years ago. Unassuming but attentive, he was sweet, and during the weekend, when we all hung out together, I started to think it was too bad I lived in New Hampshire and he lived in northern Virginia. On the last day of my trip, I grabbed Greg's cell phone from him, and I entered my name and phone number into his contact list. I didn't think he'd call me, but what's the worst that could happen?

A true gentleman, Greg was nice enough to drive me from Jim's house to the metro on his way home to Arlington, a gesture I hoped might have meant something. When we arrived, he got out of the car to open the trunk and lift my bags over to the sidewalk. He even gave me a hug by the curb. *But was this one of those "bro hugs" that guys give each other but are nothing but platonic?*

"Thanks for the lift," I said, hoping to gauge what he was thinking. I studied his face.

"No problem," he said, revealing nothing. *Damn. Okay.* I looked down to reach for the straps on my bags. "You sure you don't want me to drop you off at Union Station?" he asked.

I balked. "Uh, no," I said, too quickly. "It's okay. It's not on your way. Here is great. Thank you." I picked up my bags, turned, and rushed toward the metro escalator.

On the train that evening, I called my mother and lamented to her that I had gotten reacquainted with one of Jim's friends who I thought would be great to date. But of course he lived five hundred miles away, and so that was never going to work. My suspicion that my interest in him was unrequited grew in the weeks that followed. He never called. *Damn. Men are so dense.*

A month later, I found myself, somehow, being pulled back down to D.C.

Since my visit to see Jim in November, I had tried to forget the crazy notion I could be in med school and also date anyone. I devoted all my energy to studying for end-of-semester exams. But soon after I left D.C., Jim's super-duper-top-secret-hush-hush deployment to Iraq somehow was pushed back several months. To take advantage of his additional time in the States, he resolved to throw a huge New Year's Eve bash. Jim's the kind of guy who aspires to throw the sort of party-to-end-all-parties, and since he was leaving for a year, and since I did have this small holiday break at the end of December, Jim insisted I visit again. "You should come back," Jim wrote me in an email. I thought of Jim, and of how much danger he might soon be in, and would I ever see him again? Then I thought of Greg, and whether he might stay in D.C. for New Year's, and would I ever see him again? Jim's email continued, referencing some of our mutual friends: "Tim and Marie will be around, of course. Matt will probably be in Michigan, but Mikey will be there. So will Greg."

I booked my tickets.

I flew into Baltimore on Friday, December 29, 2006, then took an Amtrak train from there down into D.C.

Watching leafless trees fly past the scratched-up windows of the train car, I allowed a surfeit of unanswered questions to return: Was this all a complete waste of time? Why am I traveling all this way for what could end up a sad and glorified frat party? Does Greg have any idea I'm coming? Would he, in fact, even be around?

I needed to distract myself from my uneasiness, so I called Jim from the train to check in and confirm my timing to get to his house.

"Something's come up," he said.

I swallowed hard.

He told me his ultra-secret-save-the-world-from-terrorists contracting company had suddenly called him into work. "It's kind of an emergency. So, I'm out in Virginia for the rest of the afternoon and, uh, I can't pick you up."

There wasn't anything he could do about being called into work. "Okay," I said, trying to sound convincing. "It's fine. I'll figure it out." But when I ended the call with Jim, I worried I'd be wandering the streets of D.C. with all my bags and no way to get into Jim's house. Honestly, I should have expected this. My mind raced: This is just like Jim to hang me out to dry after promising he'd be able to pick me up. Just my luck. Why do I keep getting my hopes up?

I stewed in my anger and despair.

I was still fomenting my own frustration when my phone rang minutes later. I opened the flip phone and answered the call. "Hello?"

"Hey, KJ? It's Greg."

I froze. "Um, hi?"

"Hey, I was on the phone with Jim and, um, it sounded like he had to bail on picking you up at Union Station. Do you need a ride? I can meet you there when you get in and bring you wherever you need to go."

Greg was volunteering to meet up with me! I couldn't believe it.

He picked me up in his car and he got one of Jim's roommates to leave a door open. After I dropped off my bags, he offered to walk with me around Georgetown to window shop. I hadn't done that in months. I was giddy, though I tried to remain realistic. Since he was on school break, he probably just wanted to waste some free time. Maybe he's just that nice a guy, or he was doing Jim a favor. Maybe Jim, feeling guilty, sent Greg as his stand-in. No, that's not Jim's style at all. He's a great friend, but he's hardly the apologetic or considerate type. I still couldn't let myself read anything into Greg's behavior. I worked at convincing myself there was no way he might actually like me. *Silly. Women are so dense.*

For lunch, Greg took me to Pizza Paradiso on M Street, one of my favorite restaurants in Georgetown. At the end of lunch, he picked up the tab. Maybe he was interested in me. But still: *What does all this mean?*

Since I was staying with Jim, and since Greg lived nearby, we went out for dinner in town with the rest of the crew. After dinner, despite the cold air and my being in high heels, the group decided to walk home.

"Are you sure you're okay to walk in those shoes?" Greg asked after a few blocks. "We can call a cab."

I'm not one to play the distressed damsel. "It's fine," I replied. "I just want to walk quickly because it's cold." Greg offered me his blazer. I debated whether accepting it would be weak, or if his gallantry was a hint of yet another male's misogyny. But in the cold, I relented. "Sure, if you don't mind. Thank you."

I put on his blazer and looked back in the direction we had come from. The rest of the pack lagged behind. Or rather, in my eagerness to escape the cold, I had walked quite a bit ahead of everyone. Greg was the only one who kept up with me, and he didn't complain about the pace.

A whole group of people who lived right near here, yet I was the one leading the way home without really knowing where we were. It almost seemed as if the guys behind us were watching me to see if I could figure out the way back. What didn't occur to me until later was that though Greg hadn't consciously clued in his friends, they suspected his interest in me might be growing. What *was* his interest?

I looked around again. "I know we're headed the right way, but I guess I don't recognize where we are," I said, feeling a bit lost in more ways than one.

"Well, to get to dinner, we walked south, down Wisconsin. But now we're heading along Prospect before we head back up to Volta," he offered with a few hand gestures that did nothing to clarify. Aside from a few quick trips, I hadn't spent time in D.C. in years, and I hadn't exactly memorized the street names. Under the streetlights, Greg registered my confusion.

"Okay," he said. "Think of your anatomy chart. Jim's house is at the heart. We walked down toward the spleen for dinner. But then we went for drinks at the bar, which is closer to the pancreas. And from here, it's closer to walk over to the liver before heading back up."

Greg was a high school English teacher, not a medical school student. He had no reason to know anything about organs in the body. His comparison did not necessarily provide the most accurate explanation, nor was it the easiest way to explain where we were. Still, he tried to speak to me on my terms, in his best approximation of the language in which I had been completely engulfed for the past two years. It was a sweet gesture.

Somehow, he was able to empower me with a sense of location awareness, confidence, even warmth. I looked at his face and caught that same meek smile from over six years ago. I debated whether to ask him if he had learned anatomy in the past and randomly remembered it, or if he had deliberately learned it recently just in case it were to come up in a conversation with me. I decided not to push the question. I wasn't sure what I wanted his answer to be.

HOW I MET MY OTHER

At the gallbladder, we turned right and walked up alongside the inferior vena cava, then ended at the right atrium of the heart—Jim's house.

Back at the house, Jim poured a last round of drinks for the rest of the crew, told an entertaining tale of sexual exploits from the previous weekend, then turned on a loud and ridiculous action movie at the far side of the house.

Greg stayed with me. When I pulled a book of New York Times crossword puzzles out of my backpack, he lit up. "Can I work on one with you?"

"You like crosswords?"

"Absolutely," he said. "I do them all the time, almost every day." He paused a moment, then added, "I can do a Wednesday usually pretty well. Sometimes a Thursday." He gets excited about crossword puzzles? He knows the difference between a Wednesday puzzle and a Thursday?

"I usually do pretty well on a Thursday," I said, feeling incrementally more confident and comfortable.

We scanned the list of clues, and I wrote in our answers. "Eighty-one down: Times on the Thames. Five letters. Starts with the Z in ENERGIZE. I guess that's...ZULUS."

Normally, I prefer doing crosswords myself, but having a partner to work with turned out to be fun too. "Nineteen across: Chorus for *A Chorus Line* has to be ONE." We muttered aloud, half to ourselves, half to each other. "Thirty-two down: Spoon mate. Could that be DISH like from the nursery rhyme? It's either DISH or FORK. Let's see—forty-nine across: River side. That's gotta be BANK, so it's FORK."

If my hand and pencil blocked his line of sight, he turned his shoulders or lifted his head so he could see better. Clue by clue, he inched closer to me, and I turned toward him so we could both see. "Sixty-five: Conditioner companion. SHAMPOO."

Pretty soon we were snuggled up together on Jim's living room couch.

We finished the puzzle. I put the book down on the coffee table. Neither of us spoke. I wanted to say something—I wanted him to say something. Questions flooded my mind: Is this the moment? Are we going to do this? Can we be...a "thing"—or whatever—if we're five hundred miles apart? Is he waiting to say something? Why is he waiting? Does he think what I'm thinking? Does he know what I know?

Through the picture window, ambient light from street corner lampposts illuminated our faces, which outlined the slowly diminishing column of breath between us. Seconds ticked by like minutes. In his smile and his eyes, I glimpsed the future—love, pain, growth, happiness, children—a life together. It was then I knew he would be a good match for me. Only after everyone else went to sleep and we were left alone downstairs could I conceive we were at the cusp of a relationship, one that would last, and thrive, even if we were going to have to date long distance. Even if we had to fly, or drive, or take the train for the next three years.

"You know I'm going to try to kiss you," he said in a whisper.

That was when I knew everything for sure: the inching closer, and the crossword puzzle, and the anatomy chart of the streets of D.C., and the Pizza Paradiso, and the window shopping, and the car, and the phone call, and the trees outside the train window, and the second trip to D.C. in two months, and the emails, and the call on the train to my mother, and the hug outside the metro, and that whole weekend in November, and my mother's maxim of patience, and my memories of a string of failed relationships going back to college, and Greg's smile, and my introducing myself to him by the dumpster of my sorority with a clumsy handshake. It was during the puzzle that all the clues from that day and the time before finally fit together. In two days, I will have someone to kiss on New Year's Eve and not just this year, but every year for as long as we both shall live.

I whispered back, "I know."

Get an update on KJ and Greg and see pictures at www.orangeblossombooks.com

In the Cards

The Story of Cheryl and Ken
Year: 2009
By Cheryl Dougherty

At fifty-one years old, I didn't expect to lose the love of my life. I was living my youthful dream of love, family, and marriage. Widowhood was not in the picture. When life ignored my plans, I was forced into a new reality. Finding another love and soulmate two years later showed me that a new reality is not always bad. The funny thing is, I think it was in the cards all along. Fate had dealt me a hand. I simply needed to take a risk and play it.

I moved to Florida on Fourth of July weekend in 1980. After growing up in small-town Connecticut with its long, dreary winters, I was ready for someplace sunny and lively. With my studies completed and armed with my newly printed master's degree, I arrived in Daytona Beach. Daytona was a Spring Break mecca, so the job offer I received from a local college seemed perfect for me. Early on I met a guy at work who captured my attention. He was intelligent, funny, tall, southern, and a grown man unlike the boys I'd dated in college. The attraction was immediate. We were frequently at odds professionally, but his contagious laughter and quick wit kept the process fun. I looked forward to the way our eyes caught while arguing on budget items, sparkling with enthusiasm as we each tried to one-up the other. His deep voice and warm Southern drawl drew me in while his knowledge and confidence challenged me intellectually. When I was with him, I felt grown-up, appreciated, and attractive. The crush I developed for Southern Man was powerful. Although the interest was clearly mutual, his status as a divorced dad with a girlfriend kept us from exploring a relationship.

I was a single girl in a party town, and my social life was exactly as I'd expected: days at the beach, clubs with friends, sports, concerts, and hanging out with my roommate, Mary James. Mary was also single and looking for Mr. Right. While we had fun, I was secretly pining for Southern Man. Our social circle included many male friends, so we were always "safe" when hitting the clubs in a group for entertainment and dancing. Friday nights usually included a stop at the local favorite, Aku Tiki. Their house band, The Better Way, played lively dance music, and the place was always hopping.

One Friday, I parked my tan Plymouth Duster beside the giant Easter Island head in Aku Tiki's parking lot and headed for the heavy door with Mary and a few other friends.

"I bet this is the only nightclub on the beach that's in a basement!" I said as we descended the stairs to the sounds of the Kinks' *You Really Got Me*. Once our eyes adjusted to the darkness of the windowless room, we found two tables at the rear, put them together to form a long one, and ordered our first pitcher of beer.

The opening chords of *Ain't Too Proud to Beg* made me rock

in my seat. I glanced around just as a dark-haired guy rose from his seat near the stairs. He ambled across the dance floor, broad shoulders already swaying lightly to the music. Cute, I thought, then realized he was coming our way.

When he reached my table, he stopped and smiled. "Do you want to dance?"

"Sure," I said.

We took our place on the small floor in front of the bandstand. The room was too dark for me to tell his eye color, but his smile seemed genuine. I guessed him to be about six feet tall. I had a thing for tall men.

His slender frame wasn't always in sync with the beat, but he didn't seem to mind, which made it fun. Partway through, arms swinging and head bobbing, he looked at me and said, "You remind me of Sondra Locke."

I smiled and kept dancing.

"You know, Clint Eastwood's girlfriend who's in his movies."

I answered, "Oh yeah. I know who she is."

"She's blonde and pretty, just like you."

Initially, the words signaled a pick-up line. But even over the music, the tone rang warm and true. He leaned toward me, eyes crinkling. There wasn't a hint of a leer or laugh as he studied my face. I didn't sense an ulterior motive. A nice guy was paying me a genuine compliment—that stinks. If I were in the market for a date, this guy would be a REALLY good candidate. But I was carrying a torch for Southern Man. What is wrong with me? *You're only interested in a dance partner, so don't give him an opportunity to take it further.*

When the song ended, I said a quick thank you, spun toward my table, and hurried back to my friends as fast as I could without actually running across the dance floor. Nice Guy got the hint and didn't follow.

Carrying the torch for Southern Man became increasingly lonely in the following months, so I took a small step and made some casual dates. Although I didn't encounter Nice Guy again, I met Coffee Drinker for one meeting that led nowhere. Silent Sam seemed to adore me but hardly ever spoke. I don't need to say more about Man Who Wanted to be Hook-up King. Best Buddy would never be more than that. All I could think about was Southern Man.

Things eventually changed. In 1981, Southern Man's relationship ended. We had a date, then a second. It became monthly, weekly, and finally developed into something full-fledged. He was an educator and administrator, but his roots were as a rock and roll musician which made him even more attractive. We both loved classical music too. Our date night concerts ranged from Jimmy Buffett, Three Dog Night, Tina Turner, and the Beach Boys to many performances by the London Symphony Orchestra who made their summer home in Daytona.

Our connection grew and developed, and for the next twenty-six years, I enjoyed a deeply passionate, sometimes tumultuous relationship which included a brief split, a long marriage, and jointly raising his children with their mother and stepfather.

His four-year illness and eventual death in 2007 left me devastated.

After twelve months of hearing, "It gets better after the first year," I found out it wasn't a whole lot better. I'd built new routines, taken on new interests and activities, but still lived with an enormous emptiness that threatened to swallow me if I wasn't constantly vigilant. It was like an invisible vacuum cleaner hose followed close behind me, picking up bits and pieces of bitterness, negativity, and depression that randomly broke away. If I slowed down for too long, all the positives about me would also disappear into that hose, leaving just a small pile of dusty fragments on the floor.

A survivor by nature, I decided to seek assistance. Several sessions of private counseling helped a little but weren't worth the copayments not covered by insurance. Then one day as I read the local newspaper, I saw a small notice for a meeting of widowed persons in their 50s and 60s. It was sponsored by Hospice and held within a reasonable distance from home. What did I have to lose? I called the number listed in the paper and joined the group.

As I climbed the stairs to that first meeting in May 2008, I couldn't imagine the changes it would eventually bring to my life. I was nervous but optimistic when I met the fourteen men and women in the room. They were like me, frozen in the mixture of grief, fear, loneliness, and disorientation that comes from having your social, family, and friendship statuses turned upside down. This wasn't supposed to happen to people who were still young and vibrant, and it certainly wasn't supposed to happen to us.

Over the next several months, we shared stories, cried, and exchanged advice. There were late night phone calls when darkness threatened the delicately balanced new existence, and anniversaries were always treated with exceptional care. We kicked each other in the pants when the pity party dipped to nauseating lows. That's one of the advantages of a support group: you don't have to be politically correct with folks who share your pain.

Our meetings evolved.

We started having coffee afterward and eventually heading out to dinner to continue our discussions. As time progressed, the dinners included more and more laughter and became the highlight of the weekly meetings.

We were waking up again.

One evening our counselor announced it was time for her to push us out of the nest. We had accomplished our goal, formed support networks, and developed coping skills. The threshold into our new lives had been crossed.

Several of us continued to meet weekly even as our lives moved on. Most weeks, the gathering consisted of a core group of six women, so the conversations became more intimate. While sitting in a large, round booth at Ruby Tuesday one evening, the talk turned to dating. Like me, Terri had lost her soulmate after a long illness. Financially comfortable, she had clear expectations about the lifestyle she wished to continue.

"There is so much traveling ahead of me, and I really want a guy who can do it with me. But I'm retired. How in the world am I going to meet someone?" she asked as she sipped her vodka tonic.

"Well, I know exactly what I'm looking for," snorted Sarah, another group member, in her classic New Jersey accent. "Sex, baby, sex!" We responded with lots of nervous laughter and some bawdy joking.

On another night, Terri and Sarah announced they were going online in search of companionship. While most of the responses were positive, I freaked. Still madly in love with my late husband, I felt threatened by the idea of dating. I'd also read lots of horror stories about people duped by online predators.

"Remember the story we heard about the guy who accessed that woman's bank account and wiped her finances clean?" I reminded them. "And how about sexual predators? We don't know if anything posted is true. It's hard enough to know what you're getting when you meet someone face to face. I can't imagine going to a dating site." I said, shaking my head.

The girls nodded but weren't swayed.

So it began—our weekly sharing sessions focused on all new topics: Which sites are better? Should I meet this guy? Why does it make me miss my husband?

Everyone approached dating differently.

Terri was Serial Dater. She set up several meetings each week in search of someone who fit her lengthy list of specific traits. Claire's search for love attracted distant men in need of money, which she often sent despite our protests. Susan leaped into each new encounter, thus becoming Sky Diver, rarely having a first date that didn't end with sex. If a second date happened, the guy could expect to be introduced to her entire family. Thrill Seeker, Sarah, was drawn to bad boys who met her at bars. Connie remained grounded and careful. She met a few nice men for coffee or dinner but in general, took things slowly.

I was Cement Boot. I just couldn't take the step.

The shared stories were interesting and amusing.

...He writes me all these complicated poems. Half the time I don't know what the heck he's talking about.

HOW I MET MY OTHER

...My last date was at least twenty years older than his profile picture. He was on a walker, for heaven's sake.

Despite the risks and disappointments, their bubbling enthusiasm for their rejuvenated lives was infectious, and I found myself laughing to the point of tears at almost every weekly dinner.

I also felt something new.

A growing void. A feeling that something was missing. Sure, I missed my lost husband and the world we inhabited, but this was different. It wasn't specific to him. I missed the warmth and companionship, the social nature of a relationship with a man. I wasn't in the market for a husband or even love, I just wanted to have dinner and maybe dance with someone nice. At night I found myself praying to God to send me a good man who truly cared about me. It took time, but I eventually realized that I might be ready for a step forward.

My fear of Internet dating eliminated that option, so Connie suggested I dip my cement toe into the dating pool by attending a social event at our church, a buffet dinner with a band. There would be dancing.

It was time to take a shot.

The night before the dance, my nerves and emotions ran wild. I sat in my recliner stroking my cat as she purred in my lap. I felt sadness and guilt at the thought of "moving away" from my husband.

"Hi, Baby," I whispered into the room. "I know you hear me. I love you so much, and I miss you. That will never change, but it hurts to be this lonely. I don't want the rest of my life to be this way. What can I do?"

The room remained quiet.

In an attempt to distract myself from the swirl of feelings, I tuned in to the movie *Mamma Mia.* As Meryl Streep and company light-heartedly spun and sang to *Dancing Queen,* tears poured down my cheeks. Streep's character suffered loss and heartache. As a result, she locked herself away physically and emotionally. She resisted opening her heart again with all her might but took the chance.

A sob rolled up from deep in my gut. Someday I might have a similar chance. Why was I sobbing? A new chance at life would be wonderful.

Our hearts are large, complex entities. They're not balloons whose interiors are wide open space. There are numerous chambers, each one fulfilling a specific purpose. The chamber which contained my love for my husband was full and rich. That's where I've spent so many years of my life. Beside it, though, were other chambers which held new potential. If I took a step into one of those chambers, I wouldn't be losing the ties to my husband. That area would continue beating strongly. Its strength would help support those other chambers and the things that filled them. Like the blood and oxygen that flow physically back and forth in our hearts, the flow of memories and emotions make *all* the chambers stronger. I wouldn't be leaving my love. Instead, I would enhance my ties by letting my entire heart live.

I woke the next day ready for a new adventure, energized and upbeat, even optimistic. That evening Connie drove to my house, and we headed out together.

I was a bit nervous, so we joked as we made our way toward

my "baptism" into single social life. "How many of these church hall spaghetti dinners have you been to in your life?" she asked.

"Hey, I grew up Catholic," I laughed, "so it felt like I attended hundreds of them, and they're all alike. Since the beginning of time, the sauce has been bland, the cheese resembles cardboard, and the bread is incredibly dry."

She snorted as she laughed, "Yeah, that's exactly how I remember them too!"

As we entered the hall, we immediately headed to the beverage table and grabbed glasses of the cheap red wine. I relaxed a little. There was familiarity here.

Connie led the way and set her glass down at an available spot. As we settled in, we introduced ourselves to our tablemates: an elderly couple, their daughter and son-in-law, and a second older couple. Connie and I spent several cheerful minutes sharing light banter with our new acquaintances. Dinner arrived, and as I chewed on the limp white lettuce swimming in Italian dressing, I found myself relaxing and having fun.

Dessert arrived, and the band took the stage. They were surprisingly good. Couples began to fill the floor. Scanning the room, I soon realized *watching* would be our entertainment for the night, unfortunately. There were no single men anywhere. Connie and I laughed at our luck and decided to enjoy ourselves anyway.

We'd been sipping wine and chatting warmly with our new friends for about thirty minutes when something bumped my right leg. I shifted in my seat and continued talking to the couple on my left. A few moments later, I again felt something at my right leg. I turned right, met the leering gaze of "son-in-law," and realized he was trying to play footsies with me while his wife was distracted by her parents. Connie wanted to know what was going on, and I was eventually able to whisper a response. She burst into laughter, then we finished our wine, and headed home while anticipating the hilarious response we'd get when the girls heard about it at dinner the next week.

My first night out wasn't a complete disaster. In addition to reawakening my sense of humor, it made me realize there were risks everywhere, not just online. If I wanted a new life, I had to try new things. There wasn't much to lose, especially if I was careful, so I researched, made my choice, and took the plunge.

Match.com was my site.

I was skeptical and meticulous as I completed my online profile, thinking carefully before answering questions. After hearing my friends' stories, I didn't want to attract the wrong guys by putting out a vibe that wasn't accurate. My photos were attractive but not sexy. My bio included warm references to my first marriage along with my interests in music, dancing, travel, and reading.

"I'm not looking for a husband," I noted to the girls the night I shared my sample profile with them. "It would just be nice to share dinners and outings with someone interesting."

"Yeah, and I bet you'd like to share a few other things too!" Sarah said, winking.

I blushed. "Actually, that's not out of the picture either." We all laughed as they finished their critique of my Match bio.

I had several hard and fast rules: no smokers, geographically close, and no one whose status was "recently separated" or "never married." I felt that men in both categories might present issues I didn't care to address.

My page generated moderate interest. I received "winks" and even notes from interested men. I did nothing to respond. My old fears kept surfacing. These were strangers about whom I knew nothing real. How could I remain safe living alone while dating online? I considered dropping out but then remembered the only way I would heal and strengthen my heart was to open those new chambers.

Ms. Cement Foot needed to form a plan and stick to it.

The Safety Plan included not divulging my last name or number until after the first date. I wouldn't share my address until I was comfortable. Before leaving for a date, I printed the profile of my suitor, wrote down the address and time of our meeting, and posted it on my refrigerator. Then I would share all these facts with one or two friends prior to leaving and would check in when I got home. The whole prospect seemed daunting, but I pushed on.

With the Safety Plan in place, I started responding to some of the requests.

The day finally came when a seemingly nice guy invited me to lunch. I approached it with much of the same nervousness I'd felt before the church dinner dance.

"My palms are sweating, but at least I'm not crying," I said, joking to Connie on the telephone as I prepared to go.

"That dinner broke the ice," she answered. "Now get out there and embrace your new life!"

Wearing a nice pair of slacks and a blouse, my hair fixed, light makeup on my face, I arrived at the restaurant where a gentleman waited.

A police officer.

It was surprising how quickly I regained my "dating feet." My nerves weren't tearing me up inside as I'd expected. Conversation came with ease, and I relaxed enough to enjoy myself a bit. He was soft-spoken, interesting, professional, and pleasant. But not for me. I knew it within minutes. There wasn't enough "life" in him. He smiled, but he didn't laugh. Although he enjoyed his career, I didn't sense a passion for it or for anything we discussed. If I'm starting a new life, I need a companion with some life in him.

Luckily, we'd met for lunch, so it was over in a relatively brief time. When I got home, I experienced a feeling I've had hundreds of times in my life after attempting something new and frightening: I survived. *And now I know I can do it, I don't have to be scared anymore.* Later that evening he called and asked to see me again. I declined, and he reacted like the nice guy I sensed him to be.

Luckily, my first dating experience had been a good one, so I marched on.

There were others, though not many. Some for whom the emails led to a nice cup of coffee or a quick lunch. They always ended with the single date. A few didn't ask to see me again. The others, I hope, did not feel slighted when I offered my regrets. They were nice people, but not for me.

"I never knew I was so superficial," I confessed to the girls as we shared pizza one evening around Terri's kitchen table, "but I need to feel *some* physical attraction if I'm going to see someone.

That's not all of it though, that guy from Orlando was absolutely gorgeous, but he never asked me a single question about myself. All he did was brag about his job, his house, and himself in general."

"It wasn't a total loss. At least the view was good." Terri laughed. We all raised our wine glasses and toasted that one.

One afternoon in the spring of 2009 I logged on to Match to "shop" as our support group jokingly called it. While reading a message from my inbox, I noticed a profile thumbnail on the side of the page. A smiling man held a glass of wine and asked, "Are you watching that sunset too?" There was something light and bright in his demeanor. I clicked on the profile, which was upbeat and interesting. He talked about his love of golf and music. His dedication to his profession was obvious by the numerous related activities he mentioned. It was clear that he was intelligent and had a warm sense of humor. Although he said he generally ate a healthy diet, he added that "sometimes you've just got to go for that pizza!" It made me smile.

On paper, it appeared that we had several things in common. But I'd had enough experience to know the written profile doesn't tell the whole story. Chemistry involves something that doesn't translate through phone lines or Wi-Fi. As I read on, an item in the profile suddenly leaped off the page. Status: Never Married.

Rats.

Normally, I checked the status first and eliminated these without ever reading the profile. How had that gotten past me? I was about to hit the delete button but hesitated. I looked at the picture a bit longer and read the entire profile again, looking for something, perhaps another reason to justify deleting it. There wasn't one. What *was* there was a description of somebody I'd like to get to know. Without thinking too long, I moved the cursor on the page and clicked "Wink." As my wink sped through cyberspace toward Never Married's computer, I thought, so much for my rules.

He responded with a tone that reflected what I'd read in his profile. *Hey, it's great to hear from you! You're from the northeast too. How'd you end up here?* He seemed warm and interested. It was encouraging. Over the course of several increasingly long emails, I learned that he was a retired chiropractor. What more could a woman with back issues want?

Never Married let me know he was not necessarily looking for long-term commitment but sought the same type of companionship, a close friendship with someone willing to share enjoyable experiences. We talked about books, movies, music, food. Coincidentally, *The Big Chill* was a favorite we shared, both as a movie and for its soundtrack.

The movie captured the way our generation formed such close bonds in college. It reminded me of my own experience, he wrote.

I feel the same way! I thought. *This guy is interesting. I'd like to talk to him more.* When he asked me to meet him for lunch, I eagerly agreed.

The next day I arrived at Ruby Tuesday a few minutes early and followed my safety routine. I parked in an unusual location so if he turned out to be a lunatic, I could make my escape before he had the opportunity to get to his car and follow me. Then I sat on a bench in the lobby facing the door and waited. Each time the door opened, my breath caught. *Is this him?* Any noise in the parking lot behind me made me snap my head up to maybe catch a glimpse of him as he approached.

Precisely at the scheduled time, the door opened, and he stepped in. He was six feet tall, slim, with a full head of white hair. His crystal blue eyes crinkled whenever his easy smile crossed his face. I immediately renamed him, Handsome Man. Wow. This guy was even better looking in person than in his profile. *YES!* My face flushed with excitement.

"You must be Ken," I said looking up toward him.

"And you must be Cheryl," he responded. He smiled broadly, and his blue eyes twinkled.

"Our notes and phone calls have been fun, but I've wanted to sit down and share more. Have you been here before? The salad bar is great. I can make a total pig of myself." I laughed.

"Me too. There's so much to choose from." Light chatter seemed to spew spontaneously from both of us as we surveyed each other's face, smile, eyes.

After a few moments, the hostess cleared her throat and suggested we continue our conversation in a booth. We both laughed, perhaps a bit embarrassed by our mutual enthusiasm.

Two hours later, the conversation still flowed. "You said on the phone that you were raised in a Catholic family. Did you go to Catholic school?"

"Oh yeah," I laughed, placing my hands into prayer mode. "I'm a product of the nuns."

"Me too," he added, "They were tough. People who went to public school have no clue what we lived through."

"Amen." We nodded to each other while we laughed, acknowledging our shared membership in that exclusive childhood club.

As he enthusiastically shared his memories of Little League baseball and the easy way of life we enjoyed in the 50s and early 60s, I almost forgot that it was a first date. I felt as if I was talking to an old friend. Our interpretations of those days were so similar that even though he was in Queens, NY and I was in a small town in Connecticut, it was like we had been in the same neighborhood, running from yard to yard with other kids until the dusk curfew both our moms had set. We'd both taken a risk in our 20s and moved to Florida to begin our careers with neither family nor friends nearby.

"When I think back I wonder how I found the courage to do it. What a risk it was," I said.

"Me too, but I believe that I made the right move. This is my home, and I've been very happy here," he added.

"I agree," I said, and we clinked glasses as if toasting our success.

"By the way, when did you get here?" I asked.

"1980," he said.

"Really? Me too. When in 1980?"

"I got here in August."

"I moved on July 4th weekend. We practically passed each other on the interstate!" It proved to be the first of many coincidences.

I looked across the table and thought he was indeed someone I'd like to know better. He made me feel relaxed and comfortable. Although he was a successful professional and highly intelligent, he possessed a down to earth air I liked. There was no pretense. He was confident while holding on to a boyish sense of enthusiasm. Watching his relaxed stroll as he headed back to the salad bar, I again felt a comfortable familiarity. When he smiled and interacted with a man reaching for lettuce tongs, I felt sure that his niceness was not an act intended to impress me. I could tell he liked me too but realized he was an attractive single man, long established in the community. There were most likely several younger and leaner ladies with whom he spent his time. This would probably be another of my one-date experiences, although this time not by my choice. It saddened me a bit, but I felt confident that we could become friends.

As the server took the check, Handsome Man caught me totally off guard. "I'd like to see you again," he said.

My pulse quickened. "I'd like to see you too."

Whether it was the several glasses of unsweet tea or this new development, I suddenly felt an urgent need to use the restroom. I stepped away from our booth, giddy with anticipation. I glanced over my shoulder, and he was leaning out of the booth to check out my rear profile as I walked. If he leaned any further, he'd probably fall on the floor. He liked me!

We left the restaurant, and he asked to walk me to my car. I felt like a high school girl again, all fluffy and tingly inside. I was going to have a second date with a great guy. I wanted to tap my feet and skip to the car.

Despite my rules, I let him escort me.

As we walked across the lot on our way to my well-hidden vehicle, all I could think was, What am I doing? From the moment I saw his picture, this man had me breaking my own rules. *What's going on here?*

When we finally reached my car, he turned, gently cupped my chin in his hands, looked into my eyes and said, "I had a wonderful time." Then he leaned over and softly placed his lips on mine. My lips warmed and softened.

Kaboom.

He had no idea what he'd done. I had not been kissed by anyone other than my husband in nearly thirty years. The possibility of this happening had not even crossed my survivalist Cement Foot mind. I hadn't prepared for it, hadn't planned for it. In a daze, I quickly said goodbye and hopped into my vehicle. He smiled, waved, and walked away.

I started the car and grabbed the steering wheel tightly. I just received the first kiss in my new life, and I didn't feel anxious, upset, or any of the other things I expected. What flowed through me was a warmth and peace that brought tears to my eyes but not the wrenching sense of loss and change I might have anticipated.

I thought about the kiss over and over as I drove. I smiled, I tapped the steering wheel, I tapped my feet, and I smiled some more. This handsome, gentle man was opening a door for me, and it felt wonderful.

Our second date proved to be just as fun and filled with conversation as the first. Over a delicious Italian dinner and a glass of red wine in a cozy restaurant, we discovered that we knew several people in common, both personally and professionally. In fact, he shared a twenty-five-year friendship with my late husband's childhood best friend.

"Just wait until I tell him that I'm dating you," he said, eyes dancing. "He won't believe it. What a small world."

I hoped for the same goodnight kiss at the end of our date. I wasn't disappointed. It lingered and stirred feelings in me that were buried for quite some time. *Oh yes, I am indeed still alive.* The inner me rejoiced. Although I tried not to show it, beneath my fifty-something exterior, there was a teenage girl dancing, giggling, and squealing with delight.

Our relationship continued to develop steadily. We discovered that our lives had been waltzing around each other for more than a quarter century. Some of the passes were related to our common interests. We had both attended several specific performances of the London Symphony Orchestra. I like to think we might have been seated near each other.

Other connections were less easily explained. Years after my roommate and I shared a condo together, he had actually dated her for several months. *That* discovery left both of us speechless. It was too eerie.

The icing on the cake came one evening when we were talking about some of our favorite experiences in the Daytona area. I mentioned how much my friends and I loved dancing at Aku Tiki on Friday nights.

He laughed and said, "I loved that place. I didn't go every week, but my buddies and I stopped in occasionally. I remember one night, I danced with this pretty blonde girl. She reminded me of Sondra Locke. Do you remember her? She was Clint Eastwood's girlfriend for many years."

The memory of that night so long ago pushed itself out of the dusty recesses of my mind: the beat of the music, the cute, comfortable dance moves, his head leaning down as he talked to me, and my frantic escape across the dance floor.

"That was me," I gasped.

He sat up straighter, turned his head from side to side looking at me carefully, and said, "It was kind of dark, but I think you're right. I remember I thought about following you to your table, but it was obvious you weren't interested. My friend and I left right after that."

"How could I have forgotten? How could we have not recognized each other?"

"We were young," he answered. "I had a mustache, and my hair was brown. Who knows why?"

Then I wondered how many other times we might have been at the same restaurant, store, or concert. How many times we might have almost touched but were so wrapped up living our *other* lives we never noticed each other. How easily we might have finished our lives without ever actually meeting again.

If I hadn't broken the cement boot I wore, if I hadn't let go of that favorite card from the hand life had dealt and drawn a new one from the stack sitting in front of me, my heart might never have reawakened to a love that was in the cards all along.

Get an update on Cheryl and Ken and see pictures at www.orangeblossombooks.com

How Funny It Was:

Part Two

Never Feed Spaghetti to a Stray

The Story of Valerie and Justin
Year: 2015
By Valerie Willis

I am sick of being lonely. I'm at the kitchen table writing in my journal again. My best friend Karly is engaged, and I'm still here at the kitchen table. Becca is dating and landed an amazing job, while I'm dealing with Dan the failed first date who calls nonstop. I am still here at the kitchen table. My roommate moved out to live with his girlfriend, and I am still here, alone...at the kitchen table.

Slamming the journal closed, I plopped my head on top of it. I was a twenty-year-old girl alone, no boyfriend, a dead-end job working as a barista, and all my dreams crushed. The house was quiet, making it easy to hear the music blaring from the bar on the street behind.

"Forget this, I'm going to go see what band is playing over

there." I pulled myself up and headed out the kitchen door.

At this stage in my life, I rented a room in a falling apart house. The roof leaked, and the drop-down ceiling didn't hide the mess I knew existed above. The wavy floor made me feel drunk and the water heater had a leak that went on for God knows how long.

I escaped my home-sweet-home and headed across the street to the Lake Mary Pub. The music echoed through the neighborhood, and I was glad to be around other human beings.

Walking in, I found a group of twenty-somethings having a blast. A punk alternative band bounced on the tiny stage. Soon as the band took a break, I was greeted by a guy named Michael who reminded me of Kurt Cobain.

"Who are you, where'd you come from?" he said.

He marveled, and I laughed. I'm not some magical unicorn.

"Across the street, I moved here recently. It's a rundown piece of crap." I cringed. "Rent's cheap, though."

"I get that. I live on a sailboat." He nodded, knowing my plight well. "I inherited it, but it's still home. Rent's cheap there too."

He earned a smile. "Ah, a sailboat?" I stared at my coke, feeling bashful. "Do you like to fish?" I loved fishing. It was something my dad and I did often. Naturally, I always wanted to know if someone was as passionate as I was on the matter.

"Not really." My heart broke, but I still indulged in conversation.

We talked until the pub closed and decided to hang out later, exchanging numbers. A date had been set. With both of us short on funds, I offered to cook and watch a movie from the comfort of my couch.

Michael came over, but something wasn't quite right. There was touching, but no kissing. I knew he wanted to go further, as in, all the way, but I made it clear.

"I'm not going that far." And I shoved his hands off.

Mike sat through two movies, *I, Robot* and *The Last Samurai*. Again, unwelcomed hands continued, but he relented once he realized it wasn't happening for sure. Granted, we eventually fell asleep cuddling with one another. It was a snapshot of false companionship which made me realize I wanted something more secure, more concrete. I wanted the kiss and the connection, without the constant push to go further NOW.

A week after my first misadventure with Michael, I was excited to have second chance to get off on the right foot with him. My self-esteem was falling apart at this point, and I was in *desperate-for-companionship mode*. It all led me to *how I met my other*. The perfect storm would wage war, and I would never be alone again.

As the saying goes, "Be careful what you wish for." I prayed I wouldn't be alone again and I didn't see it coming.

I walked into the office to pay rent, my second date with Michael later that day.

"Hey, Valerie!" It was the landlord's daughter. She was the receptionist for both him and his wife's chiropractic office next door to the hunk of junk I rented. "Wow, you look amazing today! Are, are you wearing makeup?"

"Yeah, had to meet with the regional-corporate people today." Pulling money out of my wallet, I handed over my rent. "I suppose you might want this."

"Wait!" Jessica motioned for me to stay. "JUSTIN! JUUUUUUSTIN!"

I blinked. "Am I in trouble?"

"No, no," she snickered, "just want to introduce you two. Justin rents the place behind mine."

"Oh." A familiar face came down the hall. "Okay…"

I had been there a good three months and saw this "Justin" come and go from the chiropractor's office. From the comfort of my back porch, I would watch his big green Chevy flying in and out, leaving huge clouds of dust and dirt. Often, I would be doodling in a sketchbook when I overheard him arguing on his cell phone. He always looked angry and frustrated. I assumed he was simply a client, but now I knew he was a fellow renter as well.

"Hey, Jess, what do you want?" Justin smiled and looked relaxed compared to the moments I spied on him from the porch. "Oh, hi there."

Jessica grinned like the Cheshire Cat, "Justin, this is Valerie from next door."

"Oh God, you live in *that* place?" He cringed. "Does another girl live there with you?"

"No…" I puffed out my cheeks. Do I look that different in makeup? "I normally wear a hoodie and bandana. Not very often I dress up."

"Oh, but I swore there was a second white Mustang there."

My face flushed. Has he been watching me on my porch?

"I thought, well…I thought you had a girlfriend," he said.

I raised my hands, "No, I don't swing that way. Sarah's a co-worker. I'm a tomboy so I can see why you thought that. I get it all the time."

There was an awkward silence.

I noticed his tattoos. "I like the frog skeleton on your arm."

His eyebrows lifted and he shifted to give me a better view.

I continued, "I apprenticed at a shop for a while. That's some nice shading and line work." I came closer, taking a more observant look, "But I don't know why he would use a five round for this."

"Do you know how to do tattoos?" He pointed to his bicep, and his eyes sparkled, "I want a dart board for here."

"You play darts?" I had a cousin who was amazing at the game. He was famous for staring at you, drinking his beer, and hitting three bullseyes without looking at the board once.

"I've always wondered how to play..." We talked for a good two hours. I looked down at my watch, startled. My date with Michael, crap! I wanted to clean the house before he came over. "Oh, I need to go." I finished paying rent and turned to him. "It was nice meeting you, Justin."

"You too..."

I was out the door.

I walked into the house covering my face. Justin noticed I'd been staring at him. I'm such a weirdo. Still, it was clear we'd been paying attention to each other this whole time. I don't think either of us thought to get the other's number.

I put Justin out of my thoughts. I had someone, didn't I?

Time to prepare for my date with Michael and hopefully this

one went better than the first. Spaghetti seemed like a cheap and easy dinner. I mean, *Lady and the Tramp* made it an iconic meal for any romantic night, so where could I go wrong? Granny always said, *The way to a man's heart is through his stomach.* I learned all my cooking skills from her, and I was thankful for the talent. I took pride in my simple and tasty recipes.

I filled the large cooking pot with water, and my phone rang.

A number I didn't know appeared on the screen. "H-hello?" Was it Justin? Did Jessica give him my number? Why am I hoping it's him?

"Hey, it's Dan, Michael's friend."

I blinked.

"I felt it was only right to call you since you seemed like such a nice person."

"Okay…" My gut twisted while I stirred the noodles. "Is everything all right?"

"Michael's fine." Dan sounded frustrated. "But he plans on blowing off your date tonight. He's an asshole and a coward. Mike isn't into you, and I wanted to let you know. He has zero plans of calling or picking you up, and you deserve to be told."

I took in a deep breath, held it, and released my anger, "Tell him he better never call or contact me again. I have zero respect for douchebags who dump a chick after not putting out on the first date."

There was a short silence, but his voice had a grin to it, "So you know why. You're a smart girl. Don't be a stranger and come out to the pub again, okay?"

"Thank you, I really appreciate the call. It's better than sitting here waiting for no one." I glared at the spaghetti noodles churning in the boiling water.

"I'm sorry you had to hear it this way." He sighed. "You have a good day, take it easy, girl."

"Thanks." I hung up and carried on with my solo spaghetti dinner. Hooray! Just me and the kitchen table again.

I finished mixing the meat, sauce, and noodles. Capping it with the lid, I meandered into my room and changed into a baggy shirt with a tiger I painted on it years ago. I pulled on some men's board shorts too. I shuffled to the bathroom, washed off the makeup, and threw my hair into a ponytail. Turning out the lights, I ate in morbid silence. I sat in the darkness, depressed. I glowered at my journal as if it played some cruel part in this next failed attempt at a boyfriend. *Am I meant to be alone forever?*

A truck door shut from outside. Who on earth is in the alleyway after business hours? I tip-toed to the kitchen window. Are they stealing a car? There was my car, and behind the shed was the back end of a pick-up truck. My eyes scanned left then right. I didn't see anyone. I reached for the light switch but recoiled my fingers. First, I better see what they're doing before trying to spook them off.

I creaked open the kitchen door. I couldn't see anything—it was all black.

"Uh, hi?" The male voice rattled me, and I realized I was staring into a black shirt.

"AHHHH!" Panicking, I fell back on my butt.

"I guess you didn't hear me knock?" Justin looked baffled and amused.

HOW I MET MY OTHER

Dear God, he's going to think I'm the strangest person ever at this rate.

"I thought you were a thief!" I picked myself up, my cheeks red with embarrassment. "C-come in, sorry I screamed at you." I flipped on the porch light, muttering to myself, "Should have turned the light on, how stupid."

"What smells good?" He sniffed the air like a hound. "I thought I would ask if you wanted to join me and my friend at the bar across the street, but...is that spaghetti?" He eyed the pot, and I lifted the lid to reveal he had guessed right.

"I'll join you." One dumped me and now's my chance to make something better out of the day. "If you want some, bowls are over there. I need to change clothes anyhow."

I put on a shirt and jeans, then rolled my eyes at the makeup bag. I walked back into the kitchen. Justin devoured the bowl of spaghetti he had made himself. At least someone besides me got to eat it.

"Are we going to the pub?" I asked.

"Oh God no." He placed the bowl in the sink. "We're going across the street to the Nice'n'Easy."

It was a dive-bar in the nook of a shopping center diagonal from where I lived. Alittle longer walk, but where most of the older regulars hung out. You could say it was Lake Mary Pub's arch-rival—equally worn down. Not exactly ideal for a first date.

"I see you like the spaghetti." I shooed him away from the sink. "I'll do the dishes later, don't worry. Let's go, the bar is only open for an hour or two."

We walked into the Nice'n'Easy and headed for a table by the dartboards. Sitting at the tiny table was another shorter guy dressed in a preppy style and wearing his ball cap backward. Sighing, I knew exactly the setup I had walked into. This was his Wing Man, and I was the target. I waved and rolled with it. Boy, did they pick the wrong girl for this.

"Hi, there." I took the seat offered to me. "I'm Valerie, and you must be Justin's friend."

"I'm Lou." He eyed me, then Justin, and there it was: *Why such a homely looking chick?* He recovered and said, "You hungry?"

"No thanks." I turned back to Justin, "So are you going to show me how to play darts?"

A sparkle hit his eyes, and he flipped open his case, "You ready to learn?"

Lou slipped off during the first game—the Wing Man must order the first round of drinks to loosen the target. Game on. These guys had no idea I was the tomboy who would be the Wing Man for my male friends.

I turned to the table in time to see the bartender leave behind a drink. The sunset coloration made my lips twist in disappointment. Lou furrowed his brow, and Justin made a face as well.

"It's a Sex on the Beach," explained Wing Man Lou. "Have you had one before?"

I sighed, looking to Justin. "I take it you're normally the Wing Man." Walking over to the table I grabbed the drink, "I'll down this, but don't order anymore. I'm underage." And like that, I took it down with ease and slapped the glass on the table. "And next time, do something more original."

"Wait, you're underage?" Justin said and Lou paled.

Laughing, I waved my hand, "I turn twenty-one later this year. It's all good. I'm not a big drinker."

They relaxed, and we closed the bar down, laughing and exchanging stories. I had ruined the setup but revived it with conversation. Eventually, my dart throwing grew erratic. I would either miss the board or overshoot completely. As we walked back to my house, I noticed Justin stumbling. I winced. Drunk behavior was something I didn't like after bad experiences with my family.

"Are you too drunk to drive?" We were coming down the alley now. "You shouldn't drive like that."

"It's just down the road." He unlocked the passenger door and tossed his dart case inside. "Unless I can crash here?"

I have two locks on my bedroom door. He can crash on the couch, not my bed.

"You can sleep on the couch and sober up some." I looked at my watch, "But I'll have to kick you out in about four hours since I have to work."

He winced. "You stayed out this late even though you had to work?"

"I didn't want to be at home alone, so it was good timing on your part." Sighing, I waved for him to follow. "Come on, get some sleep before I head out."

"Where do you work?" He stumbled behind me like a curious puppy.

"Panera," I replied unlocking the door. "Let me grab you a blanket and pillow."

He grabbed the blanket and pillow and tossed them on the couch. He pulled me close, his lips puckering and my heart racing. Panic filled me, and my body acted out of reflex.

I palmed him in the face.

He laughed and fell on the couch, "What was that?"

"I...I have no idea." My cheeks were on fire. "My hand reacted. I wasn't expecting you to kiss me after calling out your Wing Man and all."

"After talking with you, I wanted to know more." His eyes were heavy, and he drifted as he cuddled the pillow. "You're so smart, and I've never met a girl quite like you."

He snored gently, and I smiled. He'd be gone when I got back from work tomorrow.

What I didn't foresee is he kept coming back.

The first week or so I thought I was being clingy since I would call, and later he would come over. Every night he crashed on my couch. He went to work and came to my place—he never went home. Like Pavlov's dogs, he always came in time for dinner. That's when I realized either the spaghetti was magical, or I had fed a stray cat—maybe both?

I kept calling him. Every day.

Was I too clingy? Needy? Or worse, desperate? Maybe he felt bad for me. Oh God, what if I'm a charity case? *Valerie, you need to get your head together.*

Naturally, I came home from work on day nine, looked at my cell phone and sighed. Today I would not be calling him. Nope, no needy, clingy Valerie. Neither of us announced to friends that we were "dating" or "boyfriend and girlfriend." Nothing but a few peck-worthy kisses had unfolded. In fact, we had mostly talked, eaten dinner, or done things we both loved like junkyard diving, mudding, fishing, and playing video games. There were no fancy restaurants, no holding hands, no looking dreamily at each other. We hung out like best buddies.

A few hours passed: no phone call. I sighed a lonesome huff. It was almost dinnertime, so I decided to start cooking. I had just mixed all the components, stirring the pot and looking sad into the swirl of tomato sauce-soaked noodles, when my back door opened.

"Hey, honey." Justin waltzed in and leaned over my shoulder with wide-eyes. "Spaghetti again!"

"Y-yeah." I flinched, not sure what was happening as he kissed my cheek and marched to the bathroom.

Looking down at my noodles, I pondered the situation. He didn't even call or text me, but he was right on time. What did that mean? Did I miss something? Were we officially a thing? Was he ever going back HOME?

On dart league nights he'd come stumbling across the street to crash here, but for the rest of the days, he was here in time for dinner, video games, and a movie before snoring on the couch. I didn't have to call anymore.

We had started seeing one another the last week of January, so Valentine's Day was approaching, and his visits weren't slowing down. Should I get him something? I mean, we were sort of dating, weren't we? He said a picture of his dog couldn't be enlarged at Walgreens. Maybe I could draw it instead.

Valentine's Day arrived, and with it, a fever and horrible sinus infection. I was at the grocery store picking up medicine while talking to him on the phone. "I'm sorry, I don't feel well."

"Babe, it's okay. Why don't we stay in like normal and you get some rest? Need anything?"

"No," I sighed, "I'll cook something hearty for cold weather. You like chili?"

"Grab some sour cream and cheese for it, and I'm sold."

Once I was home, I pounded back the plethora of medications and set out to make the chili. My mind was a complete fog, but thankfully I finished the sketch of his dog beforehand. When Justin came through the door, he found me napping in a blanket burrito on the couch. He carried a huge heart container of candy turtles and a big pink rose.

I sat up smiling, "It's a shame my nose is clogged. I would have loved to smell this."

"I stole it from my mom's bush," he confessed. "I can bring you another when you feel better."

Laughing, I pulled myself off the couch, "Let's eat." There wasn't a cloud in the sky that afternoon, and the weather was nice. "Want to sit outside?"

"Sounds like a good idea." He put the flower in a vase on the kitchen table.

I fixed us both bowls of chili and full glasses of sweet tea. "I did my best. My sinus infection is so bad I can barely taste anything."

He helped me carry everything outside. I snuggled in, eating until Justin coughed hard. Then harder. His face turned red, and he gulped down the tea. The glass was empty when it returned to the table.

I covered my face. "I over-spiced it, didn't I? You don't have to eat it, I can make you some—"

He held up his hand, "It's spicy, but..." He fought the cough for a second. "It's good, just needs a lot more sour cream.

He left and returned with a refill of sweet tea and the tub of sour cream. I watched him dump six blobs of sour cream and more cheese into his bowl.

Sweat slid down his temple as he ate my super spicy chili.

"You don't have to eat it." I swung my hand and backhanded my full glass of sweet tea. The glass rolled onto its heel with an unnatural spin and dumped into Justin's lap.

"I-AM-SO-SORRY!" I didn't know what to do or say at this point.

This Valentine's dinner went from limping to dead. Justin handled everything with pride. He cleaned up and tucked me in bed. At least he got an epic drawing of his dog.

The rash of bad luck hadn't deterred him, and I felt terrible for making him stay on the couch. My bed, two full sized beds side-by-side, was large enough for four people. And we'd spent every day together for over a month now.

"I feel bad about you sleeping on the couch..." I'm sure my face was red. "But, I suppose my bed is wide enough that you can sleep on one side. This is not an offer for sex. Nothing is going to happen. Got it?" *Good job, Val. You laid down the rules!*

With uncanny speed, he was on his feet with the television turned off. "Nothing will happen."

There it was, the sparkle in his eyes that made me flinch.

"I've got work at four in the morning," I said.

Justin threw up his hands, a smile on his face, brow raised high. "Yes, ma'am."

I was in a baggy t-shirt and men's board shorts as I slid under the covers. I kicked myself. *What were you thinking, Valerie? Of course he's going to try. That's what guys do.*

He closed the door. I couldn't see anything, but I heard footsteps approach the foot of the bed then the familiar clomping sound of boots being kicked off. Sighing, I closed my eyes.

ZZZZZIIIIIIPPPPPP! THUD.

My eyes opened again at the sound of jeans and belt hitting the floor. He took off his pants. Wait, did he go commando? No, he wouldn't.

The mattress sunk under his weight. I tensed. His arms wrapped around me and he slid right up against me. He wiggled some, making sure not one centimeter of space was left between our bodies.

OH MY GOD! HE'S NAKED! There's a naked man spooning me and is that...oh my God...

My eyes grew wide, and my face was hot enough to fry eggs. My heart raced as he nuzzled my neck, kissing it.

"I said nothing would happen!" I called out. *You completely set yourself up, moron.*

"I know." I could feel the smile on his face.

"Th-then why are you NAKED?" I wasn't sure if I wanted to hear this answer.

"I always sleep naked."

I puffed out my cheeks, "Bullshit. You've been sleeping on the couch for weeks... dressed. My answer is no."

"Can we at least snuggle?" He hugged me tighter to ensure I couldn't escape.

"Fine."

I spent that night, and several nights after, slapping his wandering hands. We began the ritual of talking in bed at night like an old couple.

Three months. That's how long it took before the night came where we couldn't contain our desire. He had stuck around, been there every day, and despite the bizarre and crazy tone of my life, he was still there.

I decided to stay at his place the following week. Four days into being there, he walked in, arms high like he just scored in a football game.

"Good news, honey! I talked to our landlord today."

I was confused. We both paid our rent this month, so what's so good?

"You're moving in this weekend, and we can save a hundred

dollars on our rent."

No, *hey Val let's move in together* discussion. Just him busting in the door declaring I was *his* new roommate. He didn't call me his girlfriend and I hadn't declared him my boyfriend, even after sleeping together. Maybe I was afraid of ruining what we had, how natural and easy we were.

I moved in over the weekend.

A few days later, when Justin was out at the pub, a call from an unfamiliar number woke me up at two in the morning.

"Valerie?" It was a female voice.

"Yes." I sat up in bed, starting to worry. "How can I help you?"

"This is Tracie, Justin's cousin." I heard Justin yelling in the background. "He's gonna need a ride home...Congratulations on your engagement?" She sounded taken aback at the news.

"We're not engaged."

Laughing, she replied, "I was starting to wonder. He definitely needs to go home."

"I'll be right there." I hung up and decided to go in my pajamas.

Walking into the Nice'n'Easy, I found Justin and his friends sitting at the bar top.

As I approached, he slurred, "I love you."

By the next January, he did propose to me. Again, no discussion, just popped the question, and I said yes.

HOW I MET MY OTHER

We've been through some pretty hard times from losing both our jobs at the same time, to cancer while I was pregnant, and more. I've had my downfalls, times where snot dripped down my face as I sobbed, times where I apologized about my bad luck, in which he replied, "It's okay honey, I don't mind starting over every year."

Despite it all, we still find ourselves at the kitchen table with our two kids and on occasion friends. My famous spaghetti is still a popular menu item, but his newfound love is my Tex Mex skillet. I've never seen someone eat so many burritos and leftovers in all my life.

Life is unpredictable, and as Granny used to say, *life will take you where you need to go, not where you want to go.*

Get an update on Valerie and Justin and see pictures at www.orangeblossombooks.com

Die Laughing

The Story of Fern and Shelby
Year: 2016
By Fern Goodman

Stretched out on the floor at the foot of a king-sized bed cleaning cat puke wasn't our usual Sunday activity. My fiancé's skittish cat hastily ate his food, then darted under the bed—right to the middle—threw up, and disappeared. My left hand held the dust ruffle up while a flashlight lay on the floor illuminating the mess. Shelby tried to scoop up the spew with a kitchen ladle and drop it on the postcard-sized piece of junk mail I tried to maneuver with my right hand.

"Hold it at a slight angle," he instructed me.

"I am."

"Let *me* hold the cardboard and you scoop."

While switching objects, we looked at each other and the absurdity of the task hit us simultaneously. First, we chuckled, then rolled onto our backs and belly laughed. Our laughter escalated to the silent, gut-aching, tear-forming, can't-take-a-breath, think-you're-going-to-die-if-you-don't-inhale, hysteria.

This wasn't the first time I thought I might die from laughing and I knew it wouldn't be the last. Our compatible sense of humor underscores how connected and in sync we are. The relationship seamlessly transitioned from dating, to cohabitation, to engagement.

Part I: Fern's Hairdresser

In July 2016, at the infamous crossroads of 'which path of life do I take now' laced with unclarity, open to options, and almost sixty, I itched to make a change. Orphaned and divorced during the same month a year earlier, I'd been entertaining myself by conversing with online male prospects. I dated regularly, searching and researching, filtering to find my true mate.

Bored with meeting dickweeds, himbos, boozy boys, and a few snoozer guys, I changed my focus to writing and hanging out with the girls. My father's inheritance money provided a small cushion to question my current employment. I made a decent salary, which included a free apartment and utilities. The job itself was more physical than mental, my body wasn't getting any younger, and the company cared more about their bottom line than their employees. Did I want to move back to my small hometown where old friends and sisters still lived or stay here where more opportunities existed? I had important choices to make.

To complicate my decision, I still responded to a few good men from a couple of websites. I needed a different approach. The forty-year age difference between my dad and his wife had lasted ten years until his death. My sister also married a younger man, thirteen years her junior. To bark up a fresher tree I visited a cougar website and exchanged emails with a mature-ish, enticing younger man. At the same time, two age-appropriate potentials entered my feminine sensory radar.

Before we even met, the younger man went from tempting to exhausting, but the other two held my interest. My hairdresser, Nicole, became my impartial sounding board and confidant. It's a recognized fact that hairdressers are issued a gag order notice when they get their license. Like a patient/doctor, lawyer/client confidentiality clause, they cannot repeat what is told to them at an appointment until death do us part. That may not actually be a thing, but I trusted her.

I filled her in on my latest activities while she stood behind me jabbing my roots with a brush.

"I have a second date with a guy named Patrick on Friday night. He's cool, cute too. Here, look at his picture." I held my phone above my head, so she could see.

"OH MY GOSH, that's Patrick, my next-door neighbor. He recently got divorced. He's a real sweet guy. Married a younger girl and has custody of their kids. She's a raging alcoholic and druggie."

"Really? That's good intel. We didn't get that far yet. I also have a coffee date with an English Professor on Saturday afternoon. I'm eager to meet him."

"Well don't lead Patrick on," said my un-happily married hairdresser.

"I'm sure he's meeting other females too."

HOW I MET MY OTHER

During my date with Patrick, I told him that his neighbor, Nicole, gave him a five-star approval rating. He opened up about his ex-wife and declared his kids were his main focus. I realized that perhaps his priority was to find a stepmother for his children, secondary to a partner for himself. At the end of the night, he told me he liked me. We made plans to see each other again on Sunday.

The next morning, I shook off guilt as I prepared for my date with the professor. Our coffee date stretched into lunch. We ate, bantered, and he laughed at my jokes. It seemed like I was auditioning for a job, but he must have liked me to listen for three hours.

On my way home, Patrick texted me he had been thinking about us. I didn't even know we were an 'us.' He didn't feel we were compatible and wished me a nice life.

That's a turnaround. I wondered if Nicole had said anything to him. When I arrived home, I sent him back a simple text: *OK U2*. Since we were only two dates in, I didn't need an explanation, and I had the good professor in the wings.

Wasting no time, I sent my Professor a thank-you text for an enjoyable afternoon. He responded posthaste.

Thank you also for a joyous afternoon. You are a delightful, intelligent lady. At this time in my life, I am looking for a solid soul connection, and I didn't sense that connection with you. Take care.

What? A solid soul connection? What a crock. Two rejections in one day. I admired their honesty about their feelings from the start, but it stung. I thought of my parents who were now together in the highlands of heaven. They must be formulating a master plan for my future happiness. I turned it over to them.

My next candidate was pictured with a cat (I favored dogs) and didn't like to text. He also stated his religion to be Jewish. Oy. My parents raised me Jewish and hoped I would marry someone of the same religion. Out of respect and the suspicion that my matchmaking parents had spiritually sent him, I gave this chap scrupulous attention. Thus far, my compatibility with Jewish men had not been favorable. It was interesting to see his answers to the site *OK Cupid's* insightful if insensitive questions. His profile didn't contain phony platitudes about walking on the beach or a boat ride at sunset. The two photos of him displayed messy, mostly dark hair, a sweater vest, one with his proud Russian Blue cat, one alone. Couldn't be photoshopped. This guy was the real deal.

For a few days, we exchanged stimulating and sincere emails. In his last message, he posed a dare that if I called him, he would serenade me. The offer intrigued me, it worth a phone call. When he realized it was me on the line, he seemed prepared to sing Nat King Cole's version of "Unforgettable." Can you spell SWOON before you hit the ground in a faint? I held it together because I was driving. I had mentioned *I* had a sultry voice, but his deep baritone had me beat. The melodious sound of his voice reminded me of the times my father sang for me. Warmth radiated from my cheeks and pooled around my heart. I never expected to have these emotions from someone I never met. I intended to meet this guy.

Through continued phone conversations we exchanged personal details. I strongly hinted to him that a brief "good night" or "thinking of you" text would help to keep him on my mind.

HOW I MET MY OTHER

We made a date for breakfast on the same Sunday I had a one-o'clock p.m. hair appointment. I wanted to blame the churning in my stomach on hunger, but I realized it was anxiety. I eyed a man carrying a bouquet of flowers as I pulled into the parking lot. One of my girlfriends told me the next date who brings me flowers would be the one. An automatic smile spread across my face, as did more reaction in my gut.

I pulled into a parking space. With little time to calm myself he appeared at my open car door, presenting me with the flowers. I started to thank him when he said, "Wait."

He cleared his throat, "I'm here to meet a lovely Hungarian girl named Fern who has enchanted me with her wit and fascinated me with her words. Would that be you?"

My mesmerized brain could only nod as he took my shaking hand and guided me into the restaurant. I relaxed a bit when we sat at our table across from each other. His New York accent and attentive confidence melted, instead of repelled me.

The waitress asked for our drink order.

"Water is fine for me."

"Me too," he said.

When she left, he asked, "You don't drink coffee?"

"No. I'm not a big coffee drinker. I drink it at home occasionally."

He looked at me with a curious admiration. "I've never met anyone who didn't drink coffee. I also only drink it at home. I love water." He reached for my hand across the table.

It was an odd link, along with the fact that we both ate the crusts of the bread and not the soft, mushy center. The date ended too quickly, smiles never leaving our faces. I wondered, a solid soul connection the good professor referred to? I rushed to my hair appointment and bounced into the salon. I suppressed thoughts of the last few hours with Shelby until the timing was right to share with Nicole.

Heck with it, once I was in the hot seat with a cape on, I blurted, "I just had breakfast with this guy and we really connected. I hate to build my hopes up...remember what happened with Patrick? I thought *we* liked each other. This feels fluid if that makes sense."

"Uh huh," she murmured, more focused on mixing my color than my chatter.

"He's a widower, lives near Winter Park somewhere. He owns a wood flooring business. Do you need any wood floors?"

Nicole spun around, "Did you say wood flooring? When did his wife die?"

"I don't know? Why?"

Nicole demanded, "Does he have a weird first name?"

"You're scaring me. No! Not again. You tell me what you think his name is."

She sat on her stool and wheeled closer to me. "Is his name Shelby?"

"Shit. Yes?"

Nicole hesitated.

My stomach barometer tightened, "Spill. Now. Please."

"His wife, Martha, was my best friend. She only died two months ago. He's a real nice guy. I used to live near them, and they would babysit my kids while I was still at work. Shelby did everything for her. I loved Martha, but she took advantage of him. I checked on him right after she died, but I haven't spoken to him lately."

A smoke bomb exploded in my head.

Part II: Shelby's Freedom

The rooms in my house were abandoned. I listened for a sound, any sound. This house became mine again after twenty years of grandkids and great grands running around, none of which were my blood. Once we got married, Martha's four children and their kids regularly occupied the house. I felt like the interloper instead of the owner. When one of her daughters lost custody of her children, we ended up raising the two girls. I wondered, was my wife's plan from the beginning to use me?

We lead separate lives. I waited until the grandkids got older to file for a divorce. Then Martha discovered she had terminal cancer. My conscience told me the decent course of action was to stay married and have one of the granddaughters with a daughter, move back in to take care of Martha. It had been the fair and civilized thing to do for her and her family.

Having been married on paper only for years now, I shouldn't feel guilty. It was time for me to find someone who cared about *me* and not my possessions.

I had no idea where to go anymore. All my old hangouts were now defunct. I had developed a rapport with the pharmacist where Martha's prescriptions were filled. When I asked her on a date, she knew Martha had just passed in May. She told me it was too soon for me to be dating. What made her the expert? She didn't even give me a chance.

I could be more observant of the women I meet on my job every day. While refinishing some quarter-sawn oak floors, I noticed the owner hovering and asking silly questions. I eventually realized she was flirting with me. I gave her long legs a closer look and found I was attracted to her.

During our second date, I informed her of my recent widower status. Her face fell. She revealed that she had crossed paths with other men freshly out of long-term relationships. That wasn't a road she cared to travel again. She suggested I check back with her in a year. I guess she thought I wanted to resew some oats first.

This dating scene had gotten difficult in twenty years. I'm a successful salesman, a humble, charming gentleman, and I had recently lost a lot of weight due to health reasons. I've been told I look good for my age. At least I learned one lesson: don't divulge my wife died only two months ago. Omission is not the same as dishonesty, mom would understand.

My buddies at the gym suggested the only way to meet girls these days—online. I was determined to give it a shot even though I'm not too tech savvy. I took my time, filled out the forms as honestly and thoughtfully as I could. Scanning a few old photos of me and my cat wasn't too difficult. Then I sat back and waited for the responses to flood in.

Lessons two and three became apparent when sixty percent of the nine women who responded were not my type, and the rest were too hot and too young to have a real interest. One even admitted she just wanted a free meal. Those young ones wanted money. I had to tweak something, so I decided to fudge my age on the site to be included in a more realistic pool of matches. One little fib didn't hurt but it still didn't produce a deluge of replies.

Lesson four: take matters into my own hands. I went phishing with my words. I commented on profiles with a sincere interest. This produced a couple of dates but nothing steady. I'm a one-woman type of man and would be discerning this time around.

I reached out to a pretty blonde lady. We corresponded back and forth a little. I got my hopes up. Her answers were smart, witty and she *declared* no children. Witty, pretty, and no kids, a trifecta in my book. When I offered her my phone number and email address, she asked me if I could send and receive texts at that number. This required diplomacy. I hated to text, but everyone else did it. I reread my email before I sent it.

Thanks so much for your email. Sorry about the text thing, I read texts but don't send them. I find it easier to talk to someone. Maybe you can convince me otherwise? I'd like you to listen to Bob James-live-Mind Games on YouTube. He's a Jazz artist. I would really like to listen with you and share the experience (I'm excited to get your feedback). Share with me any music, poetry, novels, etc. you like. I run a wood floor business, and I am one of the top professionals in my field. What type of work do you do? I too love animals. I have a Russian Blue Cat named Micah (spoiled rotten). I am very anxious to talk, write, and hopefully soon get the opportunity to meet this wickedly funny, outgoing, and so far, very sweet woman. Looking forward to any and all the above.

- SHELBY.

Later that night, I reviewed Fern's reply to my email.

I like the jam—makes me see all colors and feel warm and smooth and slink. I guess that's why they call it smooth jazz. I love the sax. My favorite book is the one I wrote. I run a storage facility as my job, but for my soul, I'm an award-winning published author. I adore wood. There's nothing as intoxicating as the smell of cut wood.

-F

She liked my two most important things, music and wood. She seemed hesitant to talk on the phone. Intrigued to hear her voice, I sweetened the pot by promising I would sing to her if she called me. One evening while catching up on estimates the ringing of my landline interrupted my train of thought. Damn phone.

"Yeah?"

"Hi. Shelby?"

"That's me. Who's this?" I didn't recognize that deep, soft voice. Then it hit me. "Is this Fern?"

"Indeed, it is. Bad time?"

"No, no. Not at all. Just finishing up some paperwork. What are you doing?"

"I'm driving. On my way to meet the girls for a movie and thought I would give you a call. And check out your singing voice."

"Oh right. I owe you a song. Do you have time?"

"Absolutely."

I didn't think about it, I sang Nat King Cole's, *Unforgettable* like my life depended on it. He's one of my favorite singers. She complimented my singing excessively. I asked her out to breakfast.

When she stepped out of her car, smiling at me, I went numb with relief. She was prettier than her pictures and the perfect height. It was sweet that she was nervous, I would calm her and be her gentle knight. We had a wonderful first date, so much in common. I had to force myself to concentrate on my food and not stare at her. I tried to convince her to stay, but she had an appointment. My hand tingled when I held hers. Something about her seemed familiar.

Our relationship sped along quickly. Fern's hairdresser had been Martha's closest friend and knew almost everything about me. I chose to confess the details surrounding my wife's death, my real age and, while in the spirit of confession, that I didn't normally date Jewish girls. At least Nicole was a good character reference for me.

Fern was different. Down to earth. It's too bad my mother hadn't met her. She would have been the one girl I dated that mom would have loved. I prayed for someone to come into my life and my mom answered me. She waved her heavenly wand and sent this angel to me. This angel who possesses genuine kindness, was giving, attentive, smart and well-traveled. I didn't want to blow it, so I held back telling Fern about my unexplained health issues.

Part III: Fern and Honesty

I listened as Nicole prattled on about Shelby's upstanding

attributes while cutting my hair. My heart soared when she spoke highly of him but was deflated that he lied about his age by ten years *and* omitted that his wife had *so recently* passed away.

That night, my laptop displayed the obituary for his wife. My mind reeled to justify his reasoning. Everyone deals with grief in their own way. That he was already dating two months after his wife passed wasn't for me to judge. What if they had a terrible marriage? Perhaps he's the type that needed to be involved in a relationship.

I could understand why he'd lie about his age. *All* my friends did. I lied about my date of birth by two years, just to be more difficult for stalkers. This combination is more acceptable than me dating a younger man. Our age difference isn't that huge, where he'd be considered a "manther."

I didn't want to suffer with another pathological liar like my Ex. On our next date to my favorite restaurant, Shelby satisfied all my concerns. He hadn't considered himself in a committed marriage for years, but out of respect, he didn't date until his wife actually passed.

This sensitive male behaved unlike any I had ever dated. He exhibited a mature self-confidence and played no head games. He was proof chivalry still lived. We had the same sarcastic humor as we volleyed one-liners back and forth. Like a pair of old jeans, with a few rips in the seams, we fit in all the right places.

They say you'll know when love happens. I invited Shelby over for his favorite meal—eggplant parmesan. Trader Joes provided me with already sliced and lightly breaded eggplant. I added goat cheese, and my special sauce. The entire day made me happy, starting with the preparations, and by nightfall, I knew. My hesitations about his age, his short time being a single man, and my future career plans, dissipated. I followed my fate.

Two months from our first online communication, I sent Shelby an email, to reveal honest impressions.

We seem to get closer and closer as adventurous and quiet days fly by us.

To elaborate about my feelings in the new days of our togetherness, I too, felt something for you. Comfort was the most outstanding feeling. Was that enough to base a relationship? Not the one I desired. Ah yes, desire. That doesn't happen until a later date. Which is a good thing because starting as friends builds a stronger foundation for a lasting relationship. Or so I've heard.

I questioned everything aloud to myself, like Tevye in Fiddler on the Roof:

> *"On one hand, we have so much in common, on the other hand, he is older, although he looks good and is in great shape. He is so secure in himself and his life; I admire that, but he is newly single and lied about his age. My father also lied about his age when wooing the woman he admired. Does this caring gentleman want a committed relationship? And dare I hope with me? On one hand, I am afraid to give way to my heart, on the other hand I want to be the one to cook and care for him."*

The night you came over for a home-cooked meal became the

turning point for me. *My desire for you freed itself, the French doors opened my heart, and your entire soul walked in. It has embodied solace, joy, and passion for us both.*

Don't cry.

Love you,

-F

I sent the email on a Monday morning, my day off. I didn't expect a response until the evening, but an hour later the water works flowed while reading his reply.

I'm sorry sweetheart, it's too late. You again touched my heart like never before, and yes precious tears of joy are drippling down my face. Yes, precious, because you are the most precious part of my life and I will always devote all of me to preserve what we share and build on it. The first time we met face-to-face, I helped you get out of your car, presented you with the flowers and then gazed into your eyes. I felt a bond between us. I also felt your fear and assured you not to be concerned with it. By the end of that special day, my head buzzed. I wasn't sure if this was just a fresh emotion due to my previous disappointments or if the door to my true innermost dreams and desires was about to be opened by God and so they could come forth. I was thankful that I was at a time in my life I recognized what is in front of me. I promised to appreciate this blessing and always will strive to do so. The more I see you and the more we share our lives together only makes me more appreciative and secure. I AM IN LOVE WITH YOU and everyone around me knows it. Even better times await in our future. TIGHT HUGS

AND SWEET, TENDER KISSES.

-SHELBY

Holy Moly, here we go. A month later I quit my job and moved in with Shelby.

Part IV: The Health Scare

Lying on top of the king-size mattress in our bedroom, I stared at the sign hanging over the headboard. *Health. Happiness. Humor.* I repeated the words over and over, willing it to be true. How did I get to this place? One week after I gave up my job and apartment to move in with this man, he's in the hospital getting blood transfusions, fighting for his life. It was a blessing I was with him to convince him to go to the hospital before he passed out.

Shelby looked tired all day. When he became weaker after dinner, he agreed to let me take him to the emergency room. The nurse told us his hemoglobin level was a six with the normal range for men being 13.5 to 17.5 grams per deciliter. According to protocol, they stuck an IV in his arm and transfused him with blood, then admitted him into a room.

I drove home alone in the dark. I forgot to leave a light on outside. Just my luck, I met this wonderful man and he's going to die on me. No. Cancel that. He will NOT die. Damn it. I needed sleep.

From under the covers my thoughts darted in all directions listening to house noises. And where was that cat? The cat hated me.

"Shelby, please be okay." I said crying aloud.

As soon as he texted me goodnight, I was able to sleep.

The next morning, I brought him a change of clothes at the hospital. His smile eased my fear. He had a terrific temperament: patient and calm. I realized there was no place I'd rather be than at his side, taking care of him. That's why our paths converged.

I learned that this hadn't been his first blood transfusion, but he didn't know why his blood count occasionally plummeted. In Shelby's mind, if it never happened again, why tell me about it? It happened twice more. The doctors said it could be his liver, his esophagus, his spleen, they didn't have the answer. Was he a heavy drinker? Did he have hepatitis C? Did bleeding run in his family?

With his consent I scheduled an appointment at Mayo Clinic in Jacksonville. Shelby's health became our priority and our bond. I suggested he stop eating meat and reduce his stress. I googled for hours and asked the doctors questions that made me sound like a medical student.

Shelby listened to my advice and depended on me. Wheeling him through the halls of the clinic, keeping track of his appointments, hotels, food, united us as soldiers against his illness. We shared a purpose and direction. For the first time in our lives we had no doubt in another person's love and devotion.

The doctors mentioned a liver transplant, but it was discovered that his condition resulted from a previous operation that healed in an environment of dissension instead of love. After six months of our loving and laughing on the outside, Shelby's organs redirected their blood flow and compensated for its medical deficiency on the inside. Our souls were a match made in heaven by our parents. The not-so-subtle mind, body, soul, and spirit connection at its finest.

Epilogue

The sum of all our relationships, long and short, led us to value this last one. Opposites don't always attract. For us, being raised with similar morals and ethics work to our advantage. We found the key to compatibility: understanding and acceptance of each other.

Meeting each other was serendipitous, of that we are sure. Life, death, hair appointments, and song, all aligned in our favor. I'm still the most precious part of his day. I know, because he told me in a text. If we can laugh over cat spew, I'm confident we will dye laughing together.

Get an update on Fern and Shelby and see pictures at www.orangeblossombooks.com

City Nights

The Story of Kerry and Anthony
Year: 2002
By Kerry Evelyn

Friday, July 26, 2002

Dear Kristina,

It's Friday night in Orlando, and I am going out! Woohoo! However, in the two and a half weeks I've been down here, I've spent nearly every cent I've saved up. Luckily, I get my first paycheck next Friday, so I'm not in dire straits yet. I wish you were here. I miss the good times with my BFF—do you think you'll come home for Christmas?

Tonight, your brother, Sharon, and Gina are taking me to Boston Lobster Feast, and then we are meeting up with some of their friends at City Walk to watch the newest Austin Powers movie. Just friends hanging around, no relationships to bog me down. I'm so excited to finally be living my dream of residing in the happiest city on earth. I want to go to Margaritaville and get an Incommunicado. Remember the party in my condo back in

Massachusetts when I made a whole bowl of it? I can't wait to taste the real thing! It will definitely be a fun night after a full day of pre-planning at my new school for the incoming fourth graders. I'm looking forward to teaching in a rural setting north of the city after spending two years in the inner city. I had no idea how rough it was just miles from where I grew up in my small-town bubble back home.

Saturday, July 27, 2002

Dear Kristina,

Girl, what a night. I'm writing this email to you at 3 a.m. because I don't want to forget any of it when I wake up. It's quite the colorful picture to paint.

First, nobody told me Boston Lobster Feast would not have fried seafood! I filled up on sub-par "chowdah," then held my nose and ate crab legs. The lobster was nothing like back home. How do they cook them here, anyway? The color is way off from when Uncle George used to boil them in his kitchen after a day in the bay. I blame your brother for my lack of proper preparation. In all his trips to visit you in New England, Erik should have warned me what I was in for. Bleh! At least the desserts were good. If anyone noticed I wasn't eating a lot of seafood, they didn't say anything.

After the thirty-dollar buffet and movie tickets, I had seven dollars left. My first stop at City Walk was the Margaritaville walk-up window, where I was more than happy to hand over the last of my cash for a strong drink to wash down my dinner. Happily buzzed after chugging half of it, I met everyone at the entrance to the movie theater, where they introduced me to the only person I hadn't met yet:

Guadalupe Fernando Hernandez.

Kristina, *do not* tell your brother he was right. He said I would either love or hate Anthony, and I found him to be the most annoying person I had ever met in my life. You know, me, I like most people and give them the benefit of the doubt. But this guy dresses like Carlton Banks, down to the tucked in polo and pleated chinos, and doesn't stop talking. Ever. Even during the movie. You know how much I hate that. I'm so easily distracted, and I have no patience for nonsense from grown-ups.

I could say Erik didn't warn me, but he did. Anthony introduced himself by sticking out his hand and telling me his name was Guadalupe Fernando Hernandez. My eyebrows reached new heights and my eyes narrowed. He pulled me in for a hug. I am not a hugger. I told him that was my first hug since I've been here.

"Want another one?" he asked.

Um, no, I thought. Not from you. And I know your name is Anthony. And did you know Guadalupe is a girl's name?

I could feel everyone's eyes on me, saw their lips twitching to see how I would react. I think I stayed pretty cool, considering.

We went in, and Anthony, Jamie, and Merrill sat in the row in front of us. Anthony unloaded his pockets, and Jamie opened her purse. Snacks galore! Apparently, these two were besties and brought their own every time. He must have turned around at least a dozen times to ask me if I wanted anything. "No!" I whispered harshly every time. You'd think he'd take a hint. I became increasingly annoyed as the movie progressed. I even tried my "teacher voice," and he still didn't take the hint. How everyone else wasn't ready to deck him, I'll never know.

Finally, the movie ended, and we split back off into our original two groups. I'm exhausted. We just got home about a half hour ago, but I wanted to write to you while it was fresh. I plan to sleep in tomorrow. All I have to do is make Jell-O shots. Your brother's 27th birthday party is going to be epic. He's got a tarp for a slip-n-slide, and he's planning to have your sister and his friends shave his head! Do you think your mom knows? Ha, ha!

Sunday, July 28, 2002 1:05am-ish

Dear Kristina,

Just sendin' a quik emal to tell you I had more than 30 jellllo shots! I won! woooohoooooooo! Anthony isn't annoying hes actlly kinda funny. Nitey nite!

Sunday, July 28, 2002 Later in the day

Dear Kristina,

Jell-O shots aren't a thing in Orlando. Sorry for the annoying email last night. I can't remember why I said Anthony was funny, but after 30-something Jell-O shots, I think I would have laughed at anything.

I made them in every color, every flavor. They were barely touched, so I took it upon myself to serve them as I circulated trying to make new friends. Most accepted one politely, but I could tell they weren't really this crowd's thing.

At one point, I ran into Sharon back in the house and asked her who might be up for a Jell-O shot challenge. She said she bet Anthony would do it. Great. The last person I wanted to compete against. I knew I would have to win. No way was this annoying dude going to best me!

I found him, and sure enough, he was in. We kept count throughout the night. By the time we got upwards of thirty each, we figured we were even.

So, I did what any self-respecting, competitive, type-A personality would do. I planned to have one after he left.

Except the man wouldn't leave.

He hung around and helped to clean up the yard. On one of his trips inside, he found me in the office while I was checking on my cat. I'd put Duchess in there before the party began so she wouldn't escape as people went in and out of the house. It turns out he's a cat person. He rescued two kittens last year. Who would have thought?

After everything outside was set, Anthony came inside with my roommates and me, and the little crowd that hadn't left yet. I sat on the loveseat with my feet up and stretched out when he decided that was where he wanted to sit. He lifted my legs, sat, and placed my legs on top of his lap.

The nerve! But he just grinned. My eyes hurt from how much I'd rolled them at him over the last twenty-four hours. Erik saw the exchange and made a comment. I can't remember what he said, but your brother seemed to be extremely amused.

I decided to be polite and let it go. I needed friends. It seemed like every other person there was an engineer of some sort. I don't understand anything they talk about, but they seem like nice people. Someone had emailed me a bunch of jokes recently, and there were a couple of engineer jokes. Maybe I'll look for some more and forward them on to them all.

I've got to get back to lesson planning for my new class. TTFN!

Monday, July 29, 2002

Dear Kristina,

The engineer jokes were effective, maybe too much so. Jamie wrote back "haha" or something. I like her a lot. Merrill thanked me for them, and Anthony said if I ever needed anything to call him. Then he gave me his number.

He seems like a decent guy. Corny yet adorable, in a strange kind of way. He's got beautiful green eyes, too. I miss having a close guy friend down here. I love you, and my other girlfriends, but a good guy friend who isn't trying to get into your pants is gold. It's good to have someone to chill with, hang with, scare off sleaze ball guys who approach with bad pickup lines, adds no pressure to become more than friends, has different perspectives on everything, likes to drive when we go out, etc. Maybe he can fill that void.

I do have to go to the mall tomorrow to return a few things. Maybe I'll see if he wants to come.

Tuesday, July 30, 2002

Dear Kristina,

Just got back from the mall with Anthony. It was so fun. He's corny and goofy. And he drove my car back to Erik's house because my driving scared him. Well, who hasn't it scared? Haha!

Wednesday, July 31, 2002

Dear Kristina,

Just a quick hello. Heading out to the Big Belly Pub for nickel beer (what exactly is that, anyway?) with roomies. It sounds like Wednesday is *the* night to go out around here. Can't stay out late though—I'm teaching workshops tomorrow for the county.

Thursday, Aug 1, 2002, Just after 2 a.m.

Dear Kristina,

Oh, man. I think I royally screwed up. Well, HE screwed up! What the heck! HE KISSED ME ON THE DANCE FLOOR AT CHILLERS! Why? Dude, I have no other friends, and when this blows over they will still be his friends, and I will have *no* friends and—ugh.

The night started so promising at the Big Belly. We were sitting, chatting, having fun. Singing along to Bon Jovi. At one point the DJ turned down the music and Anthony and I were the only ones in our group that still busted out "Livin' on a Prayer!"

HOW I MET MY OTHER

It was the beginning of a beautiful friendship, and then—

I don't know. Was I leading him on? What prompted him to do that? What happens next?

I'll write more when I get home from work. I have to get up before the sun does.

Thursday, Aug 1, 2002, 4:30 pm

Dear Kristina,

Sorry I didn't get a chance to write you back before work this morning. I'm still not sure what happened last night. I've been stewing on it all day. I was just my usual, fun self. No one has ever made a move on me before like that. In Providence or Boston, the sleazeballs come up behind you, and you have to elbow them in the gut. Anthony is not a sleazeball, and we were dancing face-to-face.

I'm heading out to the Ale House with Sharon tonight. We are meeting up with Jamie. A girls' night will be perfect.

Friday, August 2, 2002, 2am-ish

Dear Kristina,

Well, an idiot with no brain probably would have guessed that there was at least a possibility that Anthony would be at the Ale House. It's close to his work, and all the employees have today off, so why was I surprised and slightly mortified to see him there?

214

I played it cool, though. Shot some pool. Stayed calm on the outside. He offered to walk me back to my car. *What a gentlemanly thing to do,* I thought.

At my car door, he hugged me goodbye and didn't let me go. His hands clasped around my waist, and those beautiful green eyes caught mine. He leaned in for a smooch and of course I smooched back. It was light and gentle, and then he looked at me again then said, wait for it—

"Don't fall in love with me." *OhmyGod, what?* Was he joking? I don't think so. I also don't think it came from a wannabe-playa status. His eyes shimmered with something that almost made me think there might be pain in their depths. I tried hard not to laugh...it was unexpected, awkward, and bold. I tried to control my face. When I get nervous or uncomfortable, I laugh and sometimes try to joke. I could feel my face betraying me, contorting into a ridiculous grin.

He also told me he was taking me out to dinner tonight. He didn't ask, just told me, and asked me where I wanted to go. I feel prompted to go. At the very least, it's a free meal from Olive Garden. You know how I love to twirl my spaghetti.

More later.

Saturday, August 3, 2002

Dear Kristina,

I threw a knife right at his heart.

Literally.

HOW I MET MY OTHER

He took me to Chili's for Happy Hour before dinner at the OG. While we were talking, he took a dollar bill and folded it into a space shuttle and presented it to me. Who does that? I was rolling the knife over in my hand absently and somehow must have pointed it at him. Next thing I knew, it was sailing across the table and straight at his chest. It kind of just fell horizontally at him.

I was extremely apologetic and embarrassed, of course. He made a joke and suggested we move on to dinner. He excused himself to the restroom as I replayed the incident over and over.

When he returned, we left. On the way to the car, he took my hand and told me the group of young professionals at the high top next to us had been watching us and placing bets. One of the guys followed him to the men's room to get the scoop. Was this our first date or had we been together forever? And then the guy gave Anthony his number to call him tomorrow and let him know if I spent the night. OMG!

Well, I did. Don't be shocked. You know I don't like to drive at night, and he lives so far away. After a pleasant, uneventful dinner, we went back to his house and danced on the lawn and drank until the wee hours and then I crashed on the couch. No more than a smooch transpired. Sharon was a sweetheart to feed Duchess before she left for work.

Heading to a party tonight at Arup's house. Likely Anthony will be there. Stay tuned.

Sunday, August 4, 2002

Dear Kristina,

Just a quick email because Anthony is on his way over here to pick me up. I'm going to help him shovel dirt. Why you ask? Because my grandfather would not let me help shovel dirt for his driveway project before I left. He thought I would slow him down and complain too much. I am going to get it on video and prove that I'm capable. Ha! I never thought I'd look forward to the opportunity to shovel dirt. I doubt I ever will again.

The party last night was fun. It already feels like we are a pair. Some girl was trying to hit on Anthony, and he kept turning his head to look at me across the room. It felt nice. Easy.

The first day of pre-planning with the fourth grade team is tomorrow. I love how they give you a week here and not just a day! My salary is significantly lower in Florida, but I'm bringing home several hundred dollars more per paycheck. They cover medical and retirement, and with no state taxes or mandatory union "donations," I'll be caught up on my credit cards in no time. Why did you leave Florida again? Come back! Nantucket will be a frozen, miserable island once the tourists leave next month. I miss you!

Monday, August 5, 2002

Dear Kristina,

Shoveling dirt, check. First day of pre-planning, check. Long phone conversation with Anthony, check. Can't remember what we talked about. I don't really care. I like him. Still worried about the fallout, but hey, you only live once, right?

He is so unlike anyone I've ever dated. Those who shall not be named are still stuck in post-college party-mode and are okay with that. After two years of that life, I needed a change. Well, I certainly got one moving to Florida. In more ways than I could have imagined. Your brother and his crew not only have good jobs, but they have goals. They haven't forgotten how to have a good time, but they are responsible. They like to travel, go places, *do* things. Several have already bought their own homes, on their own. I feel like I'm among people who will not just become good friends but will challenge me to do more, be more, and want more.

Friday, August 9, 2002

Dear Kristina,

It's been a whirlwind of a week. Between prepping for the first day of school and trying to figure out what this thing is with Anthony, I haven't had much time to think and process. We are heading to Chillers tonight. The scene of the crime, haha! Many smooches since then. Crazy, right?

He's picking me up in a bit. Have I mentioned that I do not like his green pickup? It's seven years old, small, and you feel every bump. Maybe I'll suggest we take my car.

Saturday, August 10, 2002

Dear Kristina,

How I wish you were here! Last night was so fun, and I'm not sure where to begin. It ended on the roof at Latitudes. We were at

218

the rail looking out at the city, and he asked me if I wanted to be exclusive (who says that?) because he did. I just about melted.

I can't help but reflect how I/we got to this point. Just two weeks ago, I was single and ready to mingle, as they say. I was free to be me in a new land that demanded exploration. I don't even know yet if this is a permanent move or just temporary. A relationship was not on my radar at all. But I've got a great feeling about it.

Stay tuned!

One Year Later...

Friday, December 26, 2003

Dear Kristina,

Christmas was awful.

I laid awake all night reflecting on how bringing Anthony to Massachusetts was a bad idea. He spent the whole day deflecting the "So, do you two plan on getting married?" question in the worst way. Joking about it. He made it clear to everyone he was just thrilled with our life the way it is, how we have so much fun, why would he ever want to chain himself down?

While he slept, I cried and plotted our breakup. His stint of two weeks home and two weeks in Baltimore each month isn't up until May, and I promised him I would take care of the cats while he was away. I couldn't be with someone who didn't love me as much as I loved him, and refusing to commit so boldly and joking about it, after a year and four months of dating, was just too much to bear.

We left my grandparents' house this morning for Jackson, New Hampshire. Most awkward car ride ever. He seemed to know I was upset with him, so he didn't say anything. I certainly didn't feel like talking. We arrived at Nordic Village as the sun was setting, the gathering darkness driving my mood into even deeper gloom.

We parked at the condo and brought in all our stuff. Through the sliding glass door, the moon shone on a wooden gazebo perched on the side of the mountain.

"Let's go check it out before it gets dark," he suggested.

I heaved a sigh. "You go. I just want to go to bed." It was barely four o'clock, but I was done with this day.

"C'mon." He took my hand. "We'll be quick, I promise."

"Fine." I pulled my hat back on and zipped my jacket. He tugged me out the door. It seemed a shame to disturb the pristine blanket of moonlit snow with our boots.

I stepped up into the gazebo and walked across it, resting my forearms on the rail. I said something about getting dinner or going back in, I don't really remember. What do remember, clearly, was what he said next.

"I'd rather do this."

I turned around and gaped at him.

"Oh, my God. Oh, my God."

Kneeling before me, he held up a diamond ring.

"Will you marry me?"

"Oh, my God!" It was all I could say. I don't even remember if

I said yes! It was such a blur. I hugged him and we fell to the ground. I lost count of how many *Oh my Gods* I actually said.

He took me on a sleigh ride at Nestlenook Farm after that, and then we had dinner at Bellini's. He apologized for taking the I'll-never-get-married-speal too far and ruining my Christmas. I told him how I'd been angsting over how and when to break up with him. We had a good laugh.

I'll call you tomorrow and tell you more. Save the date for March 19th, 2005!

Get an update on Kerry and Anthony and see pictures on www.orangeblossombooks.com

How It Lasts
Through the Ages

Amazing Grace

The Story of Bud and Louise
Year: 1943
By John Hope

Late Summer 1943, Over the South Pacific

Bud woke to darkness, gasping, abdomen burning like someone had rammed a metal rod through him. His mind reeled in a memory. The sharp stench of burning oil from his P-40 Warhawk mixed with his sweat, his heart accelerated as he tightened the grip of the fighter's control stick. His equilibrium barely kept up with the spin of clouds, sun, and ocean outside his cockpit.

His radio crackled. "Bud! Bud!"

Bud craned his neck. "Jelly Bean! I've lost you." His fighter climbed, a dangerous move for his P-40. The controls shook at higher altitudes.

"Bud! He's on me, Bud!"

He winced at the sun. The blooming light. A passing of

shadows. "Jelly Bean!" He dove in a tight spin, searching through the blur of movement for this wingman.

"Bud! B–" The radio cut with the familiar boom of an exploding fuselage.

He gripped the controls tighter, tears transformed the sky into a kaleidoscope of repeating images. "Jelly Bean!"

A poof of smoke and the memory faded into nothingness.

Darkness and his abdominal burn returned. Quiet. Memory gone. He rubbed his face, hands trembling.

Distant echoing of a vehicle reached him. As the world refocused, dim light outlined the window near his bed. He kicked. The tight, starched sheets made it hard to move, but they soon loosened. He swung his legs over the side of the bed, his midsection throbbing. He touched his side. The paper-thin sheet covered his body but provided little comfort.

Metal wheels squealed against a tile floor, and hushed voices whispered. They came from the closed door behind him—a barely discernable line of light marked the bottom of the door. The passing of shadows. Shoes tapping past the room.

Bud tried to stand, but the burn in his midsection intensified. He leaned. His hand found the cool metal railing at the foot of the bed. He gripped and heaved himself up.

His sore legs wobbled. He caught the wall with his palm and peered out the window.

He was a couple stories up, gazing down onto a parking lot illuminated by a few lampposts. A single car rumbled along an aisle of vehicles and turned down a curved exit, its wheels crunching on rocky pavement.

A screech and a solid click and the room suddenly burned in brightness.

Bud winced and twisted until the pain in his side stopped him.

"I knew you'd be trouble," a female voice said from behind.

Bud attempted to turn again, this time slower. The door to his room gaped wide. A nurse dressed in all white marched straight for him. She was short, gaunt but with an intense focus that made her appear fierce.

She caught Bud, gripping his arm and lower back, as he teetered. "C'mon." She tugged. "Back to bed."

"Wha..." Bud tried to speak, but the burn in his gut sucked his words away. He shuffled his bare feet toward the bed, catching his breath. "What am I doing here?" Thinking, he remembered being ill, but the details were sketchy. He'd been shuffled from bed to bed from Guadalcanal to Australia to who knows where, from one naval vessel to the next. Even now, despite the fact he'd just been staring at a parking lot out the window, he still felt the sway of a ship.

"You need your rest." She worked him back into bed.

Bud gritted his teeth as she positioned him in place. "Where am I?"

"Balboa Hospital." She wrapped his arm in the brown strap of a Bauman meter blood pressure monitor.

"Balboa?" He stiffened. "Italian?"

She pursed her lips, pumping up the pressure monitor's black ball. "No fascists here. This is a U.S. Naval hospital. San Diego." She read the numbers off the connected gauge, a glass, vertical tube with a floating indicator. Releasing a valve, the indicator lowered until it started to bounce. She snapped up the chart hanging from the end of his bed and jotted some numbers.

"Am I alive?"

She nodded with a smirk. "Enough to annoy me."

"I thought nurses were supposed to be nice."

"Fourteen-hour shifts with you people makes nice hard to come by." She pulled out a thermometer from a pocket. "Open."

Bud opened his mouth.

She jammed it in with the gentleness of an angry sailor.

Bud coughed, choking.

"Relax," she said, patting his forehead. "You feel cool. What do you remember?"

He combed a finger through his mustache. "Uh." The thermometer bounced as he spoke. "I wemember be-ing on a sip."

"A sip?"

"A ship," he forced out.

She stared for several seconds then pulled out the glass stick from his mouth.

He touched his side. "Was I shot down?"

She shook her head. "We don't get patients who've been shot down." She paused. "Typically."

Bud silenced, realizing the stupidity of his question. He knew full well that pilots were rarely injured. They either returned to base or didn't, forever lost in a puff of smoke. Only six months into fighting missions in the Pacific theater, and already he'd lost a couple dozen friends to Zeros, his Japanese adversaries. "Yeah," he eventually said.

She grabbed his wrist, timing his heartbeats. "You had your appendix removed."

He closed his eyes, remembering. But the constant flashes of explosions cluttered his thoughts. "I remember a fever."

"You were hallucinating when they brought you in. You were in such bad shape, it's a wonder you didn't have surgery before sailing across the Pacific. My guess is you got lost in the shuffle."

"Sounds like my luck."

She angled her eyebrows. "When you arrived, you were muttering in French. Is that where—"

"No." Bud smiled. "I'd learned some French in school. I'm from Pittsburgh."

"Really?" The side of her lip upturned into a half-smirk, Bud's first indication of her being human.

Bud said, "You're from Pittsburgh."

"How'd you know?"

"Your accent. Your smile."

She took a step away from the bed. "I don't have an accent. I wasn't smiling."

"But I'm right."

She narrowed her eyes. "I knew you'd be trouble."

"Most people call me Bud."

She flipped over a page on his chart, reading. "Bud, eh?"

"And you are?"

She raised an eyebrow.

"Okay." He repositioned. "I'll just call you Beautiful."

Lowering the chart to the hook at the end of the bed, she pointed to the white stripe crossing her backward-facing nurse's hat. "I'm an officer. You're an enlisted man. No fraternizing."

"I'm a Flight Sergeant."

She crossed her arms. "Junior grade?" She said the words like they weren't worth much.

He nodded.

She shook her head. "Get some rest." She headed out the door, closing it, but not all the way. The crack of light lit the rest of the small, lonesome room that held two empty beds between his bed and the door.

He closed his eyes and drifted off.

By morning, two young men, Marines, occupied the two adjacent beds. Both Marines had portions of a leg and arm gone, and large white wraps encircling their stumps. They slept, the closer of the two breathing with a rattling wheeze.

Bud moved, then winced, the pain in his abdomen reminding him of why he was there. Struggling, he forced himself up, gripping the railing at the end of the bed. Shuffling, he worked himself toward the other beds.

Between the two, he noticed a green duffle bag and a violin case tucked along the side of one of the beds. Bud hobbled toward the case, leaned with a grunt, and picked up the instrument. With a pair of clicks, he pulled out one of the nicest violins he'd ever seen, a rich reddish brown, finely crafted body and neck, all the way to the curled scroll just past the turning pins. The gut strings were worn, well-used, but a high quality.

Bud rested the instrument on his shoulder and plucked the strings one at a time. He tuned each.

The noise woke one of the Marines. His reddened, glassy eyes caught sight of Bud. The weepy glare told Bud instantly the violin belonged to the wounded soldier. He raised the stump of his arm, looked to the stump, and then dropped it. A tear trickled from one eye.

Bud understood the Marine's pain. Years of practice, learning the violin scales and rehearsing hymns for church, the mere touch of this instrument brought Bud back to his childhood. With the Marine's loss of his arm, he would never again fully capture that part of his life, and likely would never play this violin again. Bud touched the Marine's side and nodded. Without saying a word, both men knew.

Bud pulled the bow from the case, pinching the violin between his shoulder and chin, and brought the instrument to life with the opening notes of *Amazing Grace*. He closed his eyes, recalling his boyish nervousness when he stood next to the pulpit playing this song at his grandfather's funeral, the musky leafy scent of yellow early buttercup flowers blooming outside the opened sanctuary windows. Those days felt like a hundred years ago, in the heydays of Pittsburgh's steel production when the sharp bite of burning metal whistled up and down the Monongahela River, littering doorsteps with soot dotted in shiny bits of steel stag. He used to hate sweeping the driveway and sidewalks every single morning. By the time he came back inside, his snot was black and breakfast tasted bland with a flavor of earthy slush. He knew even then he wanted to live in the sky, be a pilot, and taste the fresh flavor of puffy white clouds. How would he know that such a dream would draw him into the vacuum of war?

Bud lingered on *Amazing Grace*'s final notes as he reopened his teary eyes.

The Marine was asleep, but with a serene smile.

An echoing clamor of applause filled the room.

Bud shot his attention to outside the hospital room door.

A crowd of nurses and patients on crutches clapped and whistled their approval of Bud's performance.

"Okay, okay," a familiar female voice spoke. "Break it up. Show's over."

The crowd dispersed, leaving behind the same short, thin nurse who'd taken Bud's vitals the night before. She stepped into the room and stopped, shaking her head. "Out of bed again?"

"Hello, Beautiful."

She stepped forward. "That's Lieutenant Critchfield." She held out a hand. "Violin."

He handed her the instrument and bow. "I was just—"

"I know what you were doing." She slipped the violin into its case and clamped it shut.

"Why do you have to be so heartless?"

She tucked the case next to the bed. "I have a job to do. If I were emotional with every patient they shove in front of us, I would've cracked long ago." She gripped Bud's arm. "Move." She forced him back into bed and tucked the sheet over him tightly.

Bud smirked. "No kiss goodnight?"

She narrowed her eyes and stepped to the door. She stopped.

Bud waited, wondering what else he might have done to get on her nerves.

She spun back, marched up to his bed, and leaned in.

Bud held his breath.

She whispered, "I love *Amazing Grace*." She winked.

Bud breathed.

She hurried out.

Two weeks later, Bud sat on a barstool a few miles from Balboa Hospital in downtown San Diego. He leaned an elbow on the counter.

The overweight bartender approached, with a misaligned glass eye that made him appear cross-eyed. "What'll it be?"

Bud tipped up his Army dress hat. "A Bud for a Bud." He thumbed at himself.

The bartender grabbed a glass, filled it from a tap behind him, and sat it on the bar. He lumbered off.

Bud sipped and breathed a sigh of relief. No longer dressed in a hospital gown, he patted down his khaki dress shirt and tie. His Army green jacket felt rightly stiffened in starch and was adorned with his newly earned Flight Sergeant blue pickle insignia on each collar. The formality of his clothing was somehow comforting.

He closed his eyes as "Boogie Woogie Bugle Boy" by the Andrews Sisters bounced from a jukebox. It had been too long since he last enjoyed happy hour in an American bar. In the south Pacific, to appeal to the sudden influx of young American troops, locals built make-shift huts and sold American-receipt whiskeys and other spirits that amounted to bad moonshining. After a couple of drinks, Bud and his fellow pilots would be leaning over tree stumps puking their guts out. Such experiences were fun to look back on and laugh. But he yearned to return. The longer he was away, the more guilt set in. His comrades were flying and dying while he wasted away days swimming laps in the hospital's pool, occasionally serenading the suffering patients with a hymn on his newly acquired violin. The Marine he played for asked him to keep it, provided he continued playing for others.

"What are you doing out of your room?"

Bud spun around.

Lieutenant Critchfield stood, arms folded. For the first time since he met her, she was not in her white and gray nurse's uniform. She wore a light blue dress and carried a white purse on her right shoulder. She had no nurse's cap today, her light brown hair with a hint of red was exposed, curled, and swept up like Judy Garland's. She shook her head. "I knew you'd be trouble."

Bud smiled and swung his hand above the open stool next to him. "C'mon. I'll buy you a drink."

"You haven't been given leave. How'd you get here?"

Bud sipped his beer and shrugged. "I met the nicest delivery man I've ever known. Artie. Seemed like the least I could do was keep him company in his big empty cab while he drove downtown."

"Great." She sat on the stool next to him. "Now you're paying off delivery men. Do you realize what the report's going to look like when I explain to the on-shift nurse why you're AWOL?"

"Aww, you don't have to go to all that trouble over me."

She leaned an elbow on the bar. "You pilots are all alike. Cocky. Self-centered. You think you can get away with anything."

Bud's eyebrows furled. "Self-centered?"

She pursed her lips. "Okay. Maybe not self-centered." She shook a finger at him. "That violin business is your saving grace."

"Business? I'm just entertaining the troops."

She tapped her chin. "I wouldn't be surprised if you were pocketing a few tips here and there."

"Tips? What do you take me for?"

"An entrepreneur."

He smirked. "Well... you may be right about that. I've earned a few nickels as a kid selling door-to-door coal that I picked up off the railroad tracks."

"And I bet you threw in a few railroad ballast rocks."

He winked. "If they didn't notice."

She scowled at him, but the upturned curve of her lips showed she was enjoying this conversation.

Bud smiled.

She grabbed Bud's beer. "What are you drinking?" Before he could answer, she sipped. "Budweiser. I'll take one."

Bud raised a finger toward the bartender. "Another one."

She repositioned on the barstool.

"So what's your name, Beautiful?"

"You know it. Lieutenant—"

"No, no. Your first name."

She angled her head as if trying to determine if he was worth it. "Louise."

Bud smiled, relaxing his shoulders. "Louise. It's a lovely name."

"Yeah, well—"

Before Louise could finish, a pair of girls approached from behind and sat on the other side of Bud, laughing and slapping the bar as if one had just told the punchline to a joke. Both wore dirtied blue jumpsuits, and their faces were scuffed with lines of dried grease. Aside from their filth, they were gorgeous, bright eyes, crisp blond curls, and perfect teeth. The freckled one called, "Hey, Joey. Two."

The bartender poured and handed them their drinks without further instruction.

Bud said, "Hey, pal. How 'bout that second beer?"

He said, "You haven't finished the first."

"It's for my lady friend, here."

The bartender grumbled and filled a second glass. Bud had been picking up hints of snobbery from this man since he entered the bar. Seemed odd.

Louise took the glass and sipped, but she was noticeably

discomfited since the girls invaded their space.

The freckled girl turned to Bud. "Oh. You're a pilot." She placed a hand on the silver Army Air Corps wings pinned on his lapel.

"Yes." Bud shrugged, taking a sip.

The dark-haired girl spoke, her eyes lighting up. "Oooo. How many Japs have you shot down?"

"Yeah," the freckled girl said. "Do they squeal when they die? I heard Japs squeal when they die."

Bud, visibly agitated, sipped more beer and turned away, brow furling.

The girls hopped off their stools and crowded Bud, petting his arms and giggling like a pair of giddy school girls. "What kind of plane do you have?"

Bud squeezed out a silent burp. "Uh... a P-40."

"A Warhawk," the freckled girl said in a giddy shriek. "I love the shark mouth on those planes."

The dark-haired girl asked, "So, how many Japs have you killed?"

"I... I don't want to talk about it." Bud spoke in rapid fire, hiding half his words in the rim of his glass. He blinked, and the flashes of gunfire flickered in his memory. He flinched.

The freckled girl gripped his arm. "C'mon. Dance with me."

"No, me first," the dark-haired girl said.

"I asked first. You're next."

Louise, at last, stepped off her stool and barged through the two girls. She was shorter than the younger girls, but her boldness made the girls back a step. "Look, Rosies. This one's with me." She gripped his arm. "C'mon, Bud."

Bud slipped off his stool and allowed Louise to drag him from the bar to a square of open space devoid of tables. The two positioned one hand on the other's hip and the other hand in hand. They swayed as Glen Miller's *Moonlight Serenade* played on the jukebox.

Bud glanced at the girls still at the bar. They stood arms-folded with scowls, pouting. He said, "Thanks."

"Obviously, you needed a little rescuing from those pairs of scissor legs."

Bud puffed out a chuckle through his nose, tickling his mustache.

"What?" she asked.

"I've never met a girl like you."

Her face softened.

Bud continued, "But, I guess you've known plenty of me. Just one of the many cocky pilots who think they know better."

"At least you know yourself."

Bud laughed.

Louise joined in, her laugh sounding like a high-pitched cackle.

Bud nodded. "Guess I am who I am."

The gentle rock of their bodies casted altering shadows across her face, making her teeth sparkle at times. Louise spoke in tones warmer than Bud had ever heard before. "I love *Moonlight*

Serenade."

Bud had almost forgotten that music was playing. The song concluded, but the two kept swaying as if the melody still hung heavy in the air. A few jukebox clicks later, and Les Brown's *Sentimental Journey* started. After the long instrumental lead-in, Bud smiled and sang along with Doris Day, "Gonna take a sentimental..."

"Stop."

"What? Don't you like my singing?"

"You're liable to start something."

He leaned closer. "Maybe that's what I want." He closed his eyes.

A violent hand gripped Bud's shoulder and spun him around. He stumbled and steadied himself, now standing face-to-face with a brawny officer still in uniform.

The man barked, "Hey. You're no officer."

Louise tried to force herself between the two. "Vic. Relax."

Vic pushed her away and jammed a finger into Bud's chest. "You're the guy from the east wing who keeps playing the violin, ain't ya?"

"Well, yeah."

He stepped closer.

Bud stepped back.

"This is an officer's bar. You ain't no officer."

Bud straightened his chest. "Flight Sergeant." He tried to make it sound important.

Vic flicked the blue oval-shaped badge on Bud's shoulder. "Blue pickle." He puffed out a *tsk* of disgust. "You're just a junior grade." He thumbed toward Louise. "She outranks you, buddy. No fraternizing or I'm calling the MPs on you."

"Look," Bud started. "I just came here for a drink. Let me buy you one and—"

Vic punched Bud.

Bud hit the floor.

Louise screamed, "What was that for?"

Bud rubbed his face. Vic towered over him and slowly came back into focus, his hand still gripped in a tight fist.

Vic said, "I don't need no drink from some chump. Now git or I'll have you hauled out."

Bud leapt to his feet and came after him swinging. He landed the first punch, but Vic dodged and punched back.

"Stop!" Louise screeched.

Bud swung.

Vic caught his fist and punched once, then twice.

Bud stumbled back and hit the floor. He tried to stand, but his gut seared with pain and he felt a grip on his elbow. He looked up. Louise held his arm, her normally hard stare was weak and pleading. For a moment, the look felt more powerful than her hardnosed nurse's countenance. Bud turned to Vic.

The bulging man glared, body rocking, waiting for a chance for another swing at Bud.

Bud stood, stepped to the side, bent, and picked up his fallen hat. His abdomen burned. He grimaced on his way up, hand gripping his side. With a solid eye-lock on Vic, Bud turned for the door.

Vic nodded, as if confirming his victory. "Don't come back 'less you're an officer who knows sacrifice."

Bud stopped. He spun. "Sacrifice?"

"You enlisted people don't know. Think you're all heroes. Officers sacrifice a lot for you chumps."

Bud's friend, Jelly Bean, filled his mind. He thought of their laughs. He remembered their quiet moments lying in South Pacific, jungle tents, and talks about home while secretly fearing their own mortality. He remembered the times they chatted about their dreams of the future—marriage and kids. Bud recalled the moment Jelly Bean was killed, lost forever in the skies above the South Pacific. Bud breathed, gripping his fists. "I know something about sacrifice."

Vic stepped closer, his wide chest huffed. "Hogwash."

Bud attacked, shoving him against a pair of empty tables. A nearby woman screamed and leapt out of the way. Bud and Vic threw punches. Louise yelled for them to stop.

In less than a minute, Bud was curled on the dance floor, face bloodied and gripping his throbbing gut.

Vic stood over him, breathing heavily. "I hope you learned your lesson, boy." He swaggered off.

Louise dove to Bud's side. She brushed his forehead, pursing her lips. "I knew you'd be trouble."

HOW I MET MY OTHER

Bud lay in his hospital bed, gazing out the open window. Sun shining, he heard the rumble of cars passing and the distant chatter of people down the hall. A sharp squealing metal-on-tile caught his attention.

A nurse Bud didn't know pushed one of the Marines who'd slept in the adjacent bed through the door in a wheelchair. She helped the crippled soldier into bed and pushed the chair aside. She stepped to the end of Bud's bed and grabbed his chart. "Have you done your exercises today, Mr. Herbert Coo?"

"The name's Bud."

She tightened her look. "Have you done them?"

He rubbed his face, still swollen from the bar fight. "I'm not up to snuff this morning."

"I heard about that. You're lucky they didn't Court-martial you."

"Where's Louise?"

She frowned. "Louise?"

"Lieutenant Critchfield."

She nodded. "We swapped areas. She's working the north wing."

Bud looked to the door.

The nurse returned Bud's chart to the bed and touched his leg. She raised an eyebrow, as if understanding Bud's angst. "Follow the hall to the circular desk, then veer right." She winked and stepped out.

Bud waited a minute before hoisting himself out of bed.

He found Louise in a room of a sleeping sailor.

She hovered over the unknown man, taking his vitals.

Bud waited at the door.

Louise updated the sailor's chart and stepped to the door, not noticing Bud until she practically walked into him.

"Oh," she said, then let out a soft huff, angling around him.

"Louise..." He struggled to keep up.

"That's Lieutenant Critchfield." She didn't slow down.

Bud grabbed her arm. "What's wrong? Why the cold shoulder?"

Her sharp eyes shot back and forth, as if searching for eavesdropping passersby. She snatched Bud's wrist and dragged him into a nearby office, shutting the door. The office was tiny, a closet really, just enough space for a rectangular metal desk and chair. Bud and Louise stood close.

"Bud," she spoke harshly and fast. "Come to your senses. What happened in the bar was just a start. Vic is a creep, but he's not the only one. We can't see each other. I'm an O-3. You're a—"

Bud's lips planted on hers.

Her eyes grew huge, her hands straightened and stiffened, and she held her breath.

He cupped the sides of her face with his hands.

She rose to her toes.

Bud sunk back, still holding her face, the lingering taste of her last cigarette fresh in his mouth.

Louise remained fixed, staring.

Bud waited.

Louise at last breathed. "Well, maybe... maybe we can work something out."

Bud smiled and kissed her again.

Four Years Later, Two Days Before Christmas

Louise lay on a hospital bed, her baby daughter cradled in thin arms, sweat beaded at her temples, yet outside snow tapped softly against the window sill.

"Hello, Beautiful." Bud stood at the opened door to the room, nurses shuffling behind him.

"Come meet your baby girl."

Bud stepped in, violin in hand.

Louise noticed the instrument. "Put that thing down."

He sat on the side of the bed with a soft smile. "I think you two can stomach a little serenading." He brushed a finger along the baby's cheek. The touch felt electric. In an instant, his chest tightened and eyes glassed.

"Are those tears?" Louise asked.

Bud brushed his face, smiling. Even now, having just given birth to their first child, Louise blew him away with her grit. The war had ended, and he was now in the midst of a startup charter air service with his brother. But he and Louise had opted to marry during the war. To do so, Louise resigned from the Navy to avoid fraternizing restrictions. As much as he gave of himself to the war, and to Louise, his efforts paled in comparison to her tenacious personality, her strength.

The baby stirred, but her puffy eyes remained closed. Louise kissed her forehead.

A round nurse waddled in, carrying a clipboard. "Hello, Mommy. Is this Daddy?"

Bud nodded, standing.

The nurse asked, "So what's the name of Baby Coo?"

Bud looked to Louise. Though it'd been years since they met, Balboa Hospital felt fresh in his memory. Louise's stanchness. Her beauty. "I picked a name that means *strong* in Italian."

Louise's head rose, obviously a little surprised that he picked a name without speaking with her first.

"What's the name?" the nurse asked, lifting a clipboard and ready to write.

Bud smiled. "Carolyn. Carolyn Louise Coo."

The nurse smiled. "I love it."

Without another word, Bud raised the violin to his shoulder and chin and played the opening notes to *Amazing Grace*.

Louise smiled, swayed her baby to the rhythm of the music, and shook her head. "I knew you'd be trouble."

Get an update on Bud and Louise and see pictures at www.orangeblossombooks.com

Two Hungarian Doves

The Story of Julianna and Janos
Year: 1905
By Jasmine Tritten

Bodrog Szentes, Hungary was built around a white stucco church. In this reformed Protestant church, most of the residents gathered every Sunday morning for service. Since childhood, Julianna and Janos had attended each with their father and mother and been aware of each other. Now they were teenagers. Janos' love for singing brought him into the choir, where he was able to exercise his brilliant voice to the joy of everyone.

This Easter Sunday was different from any other time he had been in the house of God. Upstairs on the second floor, he sat with the choir and watched the people below as they entered the holy space. The most beautiful girl he had ever seen walked in the door, down the aisle, and sat next to her family. Janos leaned forward across the wooden banister in awe. She wore a white embroidered blouse and a full colorful skirt topped with a small white apron. A white bonnet covered part of her thick dark brown locks. He knew in an instant this was the girl he was going to marry. But the parents of Julianna were wealthy landowners, whereas the parents of Janos worked as field hands.

After the service, Janos went downstairs to look for her, but she had already left with her parents. All week long the vision of her beauty was all he could think about.

The following Sunday in church, his vision materialized. As if in a trance, he walked towards her while her parents were busy talking with somebody else. He gently took her hand saying, "Hi Julianna. You look so beautiful today."

He kept holding her hand. "Would you like to go for a walk with me one day?"

She looked up into his dark eyes. "Yes Janos, I would like that."

"How about we meet Wednesday after school at the market?"

From that time on they met every Wednesday after school. Each time they connected, their love for each other grew stronger.

One day they played hide and seek in the lush garden near Julianna's home. Her shoe came off while she hurried behind some bushes and strands of her long, dark brown, curly hair caught in a thorny branch.

"I see you," Janos said, following her into the shade behind the foliage. He grabbed hold of her tiny waist. He ran his fingers through her hair, untangling it from the twig. Drawn to her like a magnet to steel, he brought her close to his throbbing chest. Their flaming lips melted together in pure bliss. She pulled away from his tight grip.

"My father will kill you if he sees us!"

"I don't care. I love you. You belong to me no matter what happens. All I can think of is I want to be with you always, forever, and I don't care what anybody says." He put his arms around her and gazed into her hazel brown eyes.

"I love everything about you, your hair, your face, every part of you." He kissed her on the cheek.

Blushing, she pushed him away with a smile.

"I must go now, Janos." She leaned forward to pick up her shoe, fitting it on her petite foot. "Now that school is finished, how long do you think we can keep meeting like this without my parents finding out?"

"Until the end of eternity," he replied. "Before you go, Julianna, here is a present for you. Open your hand."

Out of his pocket, he pulled a small, reddish colored stone and placed it with tenderness in her left hand. She gazed at the precious gift, and a huge smile lit up her face.

"A little heart-shaped stone, how beautiful." She touched it. "So smooth and soft, I love it. Thank you, Janos." She held the magical present close to her heart. "I shall treasure it forever and think of you every time I hold it in my hand."

She reached over, kissed his lips and left holding the little stone tight in her fist. She rushed through the narrow streets past the Protestant church towards her home behind tall trees, green grass and flowers. She went straight into her bedroom and gently placed her present from Janos in a tiny jewelry box next to her bed.

People gossip in small country towns, so it wasn't long before

Julianna's parents found out about her secret love affair. Her father, a well-dressed landowner with a stiff upper lip, had clear future plans for his beautiful daughter. When he discovered which young man his beloved offspring had fallen in love with, he fumed so much that the tips of his well-groomed, curved mustache twitched. Right away he asked Janos over to discuss the pressing matter of the premature relationship.

Julianna didn't know about the meeting.

Janos arrived at the wealthy home of Julianna dressed in his normal work clothes. Julianna's father opened the door in a jerky motion holding a shotgun in his other hand. His face was red as paprika, and his eyes squeezed tight. He looked up and down at the young man standing in front of him.

Before Janos got a chance to explain anything, Julianna's father pointed the gun at his belly, and shouted, "If you ever get near my daughter again, I'll shoot you!"

As if struck, Janos stumbled backward, shaking from head to toe. He ran as fast as his legs could move him. Once he was home, Janos snuck past his parents and crumbled on his bed. What transpired could not be shared with anyone.

For a couple of weeks, Julianna didn't see Janos. One Sunday morning in church her eyes wandered up and down the aisles, right and left, but he was still nowhere in sight. Her breath accelerated, and she asked a friend, "Where is Janos? Have you seen him? I don't know where he is. I haven't seen him for a while."

Her friend replied, "The War has begun, and Janos departed together with several other young men from our town to fight someplace in Europe."

"What? He can't be gone. I never got a chance to say goodbye."

Julianna dropped her head and closed her eyes briefly before rushing to the secret place near her home where she and Janos used to meet. Tears cascaded down her cheeks and soaked the front of her clothes. From the pocket in her pale blue dress, she took out the small heart-shaped stone. She clenched the treasure so hard in her hand that the knuckles whitened. While lifting the precious gift close to her bosom, his words reverberated nonstop in her head:

I love you forever. You belong to me no matter what happens.

Like in a song, the phrase stuck in her brain. How was it possible for him to be gone when she loved him so much? It didn't seem right. She kept crying out, "Janos!" until her voice gave out and she stumbled to the ground sobbing.

The wind brushed against her cheeks and awakened her from the despair. If only it were a dream. Janos really was gone. She got up from the ground and clutched the reddish stone. After straightening out her dress, she hurried home to the jewelry box near her bed. She kissed the precious gift and put it back in the box.

Cross-stitching and cooking gave her pleasure and comfort. It also helped her take her mind off thinking about Janos. Since she was a little girl, her grandmother had taught her how to embroider. Like culinary art, it was part of the Hungarian culture. The color red appealed to her, so she elected to use that color thread for her work. The warm hue was invigorating. Her shoulders relaxed and her anguish vanished soon after she began on the designated pillowcase, a gift for a family member.

HOW I MET MY OTHER

While sewing, she glanced at the whitewashed wall for a moment. Her eyes focused on a large piece of embroidery depicting two gray doves facing each other on green branches with red flowers. Glass in a black frame covered the treasured work of art. A relative had embroidered this for Julianna's parents. Julianna read the large black stitched letters above and below the doves in the Hungarian language:

I love you as much as a dove loves its mate.

When she saw the writing, her thoughts instantly went to Janos. The words lingered in her mind for a while and sunk deep into her heart. Without any doubt, the two doves symbolized Janos and her.

A rumbling in the kitchen interrupted her daydreaming and reminded Julianna of the family plan to cook *krumpli haluska* the same evening. The traditional meal happened to be her favorite dish, made with potatoes, flour, eggs, butter, and cheese.

Julianna put down her sewing carefully on the table, wandered into the kitchen and saw her mother beginning to prepare for the family dinner.

"Can I help to grate the potatoes?" she offered.

"Certainly," her mother nodded while smiling.

Julianna went to work, trying to keep Janos out of her mind.

A girlfriend approached Julianna one day following the church ceremony and whispered in her ear, "Janos is dead. He was killed in the war somebody told me."

Julianna looked up with tears pouring down her cheeks," Oh no, he can't be dead!" She fell to the ground, shaking her head from side to side. "I don't believe he died. It can't be true. Oh no, no, no. We are meant to be together forever."

Her friend leaned over to comfort her.

"I can't tell my mother and father. They will never understand how I feel."

Life continued without any other problems until Julianna's parents confronted her at dinner one evening. After a full meal, her father stood up from the table and glanced in her direction.

"Julianna, your mother and I have searched for a while to find a man suitable for you to join in marriage. Now, at last, we found a nice elderly gentleman from a neighboring town we thought you might consider—Joseph Fulop. He owns a great deal of land," her father said in a formal tone.

Raising her voice, Julianna answered, "I'm not going to marry an old man."

She stared into the floor while thinking of Janos and how her parents were unable to grasp her love for him.

"Calm down. We think it would be good for the family if you married Joseph. He will be able to provide well for you in the future."

Julianna wept and lifted her head. She glared at her father, "No way will I marry him. If you make me, I'll run away."

In a huff she left the table and rushed to her room, tears trailing behind. She threw herself on her bed whispering *Janos* until exhausted. Her voice gave out and she fell asleep.

HOW I MET MY OTHER

At the time in the Austro-Hungarian Empire, many daughters were married off to older men who owned large properties. It was preferred for the young ladies to wed men in their own class. Against Julianna's wishes and in spite of tremendous resistance, her parents forced her to marry the wealthy landowner from the nearby town.

Following the wedding ceremony, she went to live with Joseph on his farm. She detested him. The large two-story house was surrounded by an enormous garden with a variety of flowers and many different kinds of fruit trees. At the far end of the property, her husband grew grapes. In the green fields were horses, cows, goats and pigs besides chickens and ducks. Julianna had everything in her life except someone she loved.

I can't stand it anymore, she thought.

One morning after a few months, she entered the kitchen and said to her husband, "I'm stepping outside for a minute and will be right back."

She never returned.

Day after day her husband waited for her, but Julianna never showed up. Nobody knew where she had gone. What happened remained a mystery for many months until one day the mailman brought her parents a letter with a foreign address.

"A letter from Julianna, I don't believe it. Oh my goodness!" her mother squealed jumping up and down. She waved her arms, trying to catch her husband's attention.

"Look! The stamp on the outside of the envelope was printed in America."

She tore open the letter and read it aloud:

17 June. 1919

Dear Father and Mother,

I have arrived in New York, and I am doing fine. Don't worry about me. My new job is cooking for the Police Commissioner of New York City. Below is my address if you want to write me.

-Julianna

Both her father and mother sat down in disbelief.

"How could she do that to us? How are we going to tell everybody in Bodrog Szentes about her escape to America and the end of her marriage in Hungary?" her mother exclaimed.

"It's too embarrassing. We'll have to keep it a secret," her father said.

Julianna's parents were shocked again not long after. A parish priest arrived at their house from a neighboring town with information about Joseph Fulop, the older husband Julianna had left. He had succumbed to Spanish influenza.

"How sad the way their marriage ended. What did we do wrong?" her father said.

"How can we explain to family and friends what happened to Julianna and her marriage to Joseph?" her mother said. They both sat in their chairs looking at each other wondering how they were going to handle the situation.

HOW I MET MY OTHER

During all this time many of the young men from Bodrog Szentes fought in the war. Some of them didn't survive. In 1918 World War I ended, and several of the soldiers returned home to their village but not Janos. His father Marcus refused to believe his son had died as they told him earlier. Determined to find him, he set out on foot to search for Janos in Austria right across the border from Hungary. He walked from one military hospital to the next hoping to find him alive.

One morning as he passed by a Catholic church next to an army hospital, he heard his son singing. He recognized the unique pitch of the voice. He didn't know where it came from but looked inside the house of God. Joyful tears rolled down his cheeks when he spotted Janos in the choir. At the end of the Mass father and son reunited and embraced while crying and laughing.

Janos's father asked, "Why is a good Protestant boy like you singing in a Catholic Mass?"

"I got wounded in the leg, and they left me with dead soldiers in a field hospital. Because shrapnel remained inside my limb, I got a bad infection, and the army doctors wanted to amputate. I refused to have my leg cut off. Luckily, one kind Catholic surgeon felt sorry for me and wanted to help. He treated me in the morgue of the military hospital. He was the one who brought me here to this church."

Touched by his son's fate, Marcus' eyes filled with tears. It was a miracle. He found his lost son. He kneeled at the altar and thanked the mighty Lord.

The time came for them to return home. Since Janos was unable to walk a long distance on his injured leg, the surgeon arranged for them both to hitch a ride in an army supply wagon.

While on their way, Janos asked, "Where is Julianna?"

"She has gone to America. She left on the boat. I don't know anything else," his father answered.

Janos' eyes widened, "Are you sure? Please tell me it's not true." Tears welled up in his eyes.

"Son, go ask the townspeople yourself," his father said.

Upon return to Bodrog Szentes, Janos went around his little town asking the same question to everyone he came across and received the same answer: "She has gone to America. She left on the boat."

"I can't believe she went away. Why did she leave?"

He was desperate and limped through his hometown for weeks gathering more information. Finally, his sister Zsofia revealed to him the truth about Julianna's loveless marriage and how she escaped.

"Julianna knew of a lady nearby who planned to leave on a boat heading for America. However, the lady had to cancel her plans because of an illness in her family. Julianna befriended her, bought her immigration papers, and assumed her identity. She went by train to Brussels and sailed to New York aboard an ocean liner," Zsofia said.

Janos thanked Zsofia for the details of Julianna's escape. He sat down on a bench shaking his head, *I don't understand how she left by herself like that. She must have been so unhappy and desperate. If only I had been there, she wouldn't have left.*

After some deep thought, he went to his parents to share the information.

"I must go and find her," he told them. "I can't stand it here without her. First I need to earn some money and also get my immigration papers. It will take a while, but I don't mind. I know some people that might help me travel to a seaport. Then I'll sail to America and look for my Julianna. I have her address, but I'm not going to write. I want to surprise her. I know she is waiting for me. It is the right thing to do. Please trust me."

His father and mother both walked over to embrace Janos. His father said, "You can stay with us. We will help you find work, so you can save up money. Hate to see you go, but we want you to be happy."

A smile came over Janos's face, "Thank you Mom and Dad."

The journey across the Atlantic Ocean was long and arduous with waves as high as two-story buildings. Janos arrived at Ellis Island exhausted. His legs shook from the trip, and he had eight dollars in his pocket. Now what? New York seemed bigger than he imagined. The enormous skyscrapers overwhelmed him. Everything was huge in this city. *Maybe I should have written to Julianna that I was coming to New York.* He fumbled at the bottom of his duffle bag for the crumpled piece of paper with Julianna's address. After asking a few people for directions, he took the trolley to his final destination and walked several blocks with uncertain steps to the designated number on the correct street.

While standing in front of the entrance to the brownstone house where Julianna lived, he looked up at the astonishing three-story building with a myriad of windows. It seemed hard to comprehend the love of his life working as a cook for the Police

Commissioner of New York City. Janos took a deep breath before walking up the many steps to the massive front door. *What if she has gotten married?* He hesitated for some minutes with an accelerating heartbeat before knocking. The door opened, and a huge man filled out the doorway.

"Who are you and what do you want?" he asked Janos.

"Is Julianna home? I'm a friend of hers," Janos answered.

"She is not here now," the man said," I am Mr. Cortright. Julianna works for me in this house. You can wait down below for her. She will be back soon." The man closed the door.

Janos's chest tightened. He rubbed the back of his neck and slowly retraced his steps downwards. Exhausted he fell asleep on the bottom step of the staircase.

Somebody shook him awake, asking, "Can I help you?" He recognized the voice and looked up at a familiar face.

"Julianna, it's you!" Janos raised himself up and put his arms around her. He held her tight for the longest time without any words and kissed her cheeks. "I have waited so long for this moment," he said.

Julianna stepped back. She was teary-eyed, and her body shook from the rush of adrenaline. She grabbed his hands, looked into his eyes, and said, "They told me you had died, but I didn't believe you were dead. I had to get away from that horrible man," she whispered in his ear. "I'm so glad you're here now."

She noticed him limping. "What happened to your leg?"

"That's a long story," he answered and tears filled his eyes. "I will tell you all about what happened at another time."

She put her arms around him, kissed him tenderly and said, "It doesn't matter, Janos. I love you as much as a dove loves its mate—and more.

The two young people in love married in New York. A year later Julianna gave birth to Yolan, my husband's mother. A mailman came to their apartment one day and delivered a long tube sent from Hungary. The return address belonged to Julianna's father. The two of them opened the tightly wrapped package. Inside the tube, they discovered a rolled up piece of linen cloth. Slowly they unrolled the cloth which revealed the Hungarian embroidery with the two doves facing each other and the words written in the Hungarian language:

I love you as much as a dove loves its mate

Julianna wept and hugged Janos. Inside the package was a letter from her father:

11 July. 1923

Dearest Julianna,

We would rather you be happy in America than see you unhappy in Hungary, and we share your joy in the birth of Yolan. Have a wonderful life!

Love from your father and mother.

Get an update on Julianna and Janos and see pictures at www.orangeblossombooks.com

The Gift of Gossamer

The Story of Jean and Sam

Year: 1952
By Arielle Haughee

Jean leaned on the register in the front of the bar, pretending she didn't realize who just went into the bathroom a few feet away from her. She needed to look busy. She rearranged the bills in the drawer the way her brother liked them and then stared ahead at the Coke signs hanging on the walls. *Earth Baby* played softly from the jukebox in the back of The Waiting Room—Bridgeport's favorite pub. Maybe Ed needed some help with serving up drinks. Just as she turned to leave, *he* came out.

Sam's face broke into a wide grin, and his light blue eyes sparkled. "Fancy meeting you here." He set his hand on the counter, the heat from his fingertips brushing hers.

"You see me here every week, Sam. Quit playing your games." Jean crossed her arms, making sure the ring on her left hand was well displayed.

"Just wanted to check in on my favorite girl."

Jean sighed. "Didn't you bring a girl in with you?" She leaned around the wall. A brunette sat alone at his usual booth. She sighed again.

"Like I said, you're my favorite."

"Goodbye, Sam."

Jean walked into the only place safe from him—the ladies' room. The sink knob twisted on with a prominent squeak. She'd have to see if one of her brothers could fix it. Surely one of the five could figure it out.

Splashing water onto her face, Jean wondered what Bob was doing. He'd been stationed in Okinawa for five months now, and it would be seven more months until he came back. He'd been gone longer than they'd been together. Jean used a towel to dry off her ring. It had been a whirlwind romance—slow music, dancing, declarations of love. At twenty, Jean had everything she dreamed of when she was a little girl. Now she just needed to wait.

She poked her head out the door. Sam was gone, but an older man stood at her register with an agitated expression. She darted back to her post, apologizing for the delay. Flustered, she dropped some of the change on the floor. Only two more hours until her shift was over and in even less time *he* would be done with his lunch.

Honeysuckle saturated the summer air from the trellis on the front porch. Jean opened the screen door and greeted her mother with a quick kiss. An envelope with a familiar scrawl sat on the table. It had been weeks since the last letter. Jean snatched her prize and raced up the stairs.

"What's going on?" Marge asked from their bed. Jean had shared a bed with her closest sister and best friend for as long as she could remember. She wouldn't have it any other way.

"A new letter from Bob," Jean said. She plopped down on the mattress and dropped her purse to the floor.

"You won't believe what happened today," Marge said, her eyes wide. "John McDermott was at the A&P, and he said hello to me." Her eyes lit like lights on a Christmas tree. He'd been her crush for a month even though she barely knew him. "He told me my dress matched the eggplant. I'm going to wear it every time I go get groceries from now on."

Jean laughed. "Sounds like you'll be doing a lot of washing."

"But it'll be worth it! I had an idea..."

Jean ran her fingers up and down the letter burning in her hands. Marge getting ideas wasn't always a good thing.

Marge scooted closer. "It might be fun to get a group of friends together and go out dancing. I really want to spend more time with John, and I noticed he's friends with that guy who always talks to you when you're working at The Waiting R—"

"Absolutely not."

Marge put her arm around Jean's shoulder and gave her best puppy dog eyes. "Please, Jean. Just one time out. That's all I'll need. Just see if Sam—that's his name, right?—would want to go out with us and bring John with him."

"That guy is a huge flirt, and I'm engaged."

"He's the only connection we have. Come on, Jean. Just one time."

"Drop it, Marge."

Jean moved away from her sister and ripped open the envelope. Bob's handwriting instantly comforted her. A little piece of him sent all the way back to her. She wanted to take her time and savor each word, but she was in such a rush for news of him that her eyes flew over the page. It was shorter than usual:

Dear Jean,

I miss you, Kitty-Kat, and I hope you are doing well. It's been lonely out here without you. The good news is there are some dance clubs nearby where I can hang out with friends, grab a few drinks, and forget about being so far from home. There are some air force ladies that join us most nights, and I was wondering if you would mind if I dance with some of the girls. There is one in particular that I get along really well with. You're welcome to go out with other guys while I am gone, too. We can have fun and not be lonely then pick back up right where we left off.

Love you to the moon and back,

Bob

The letter shook in Jean's hands. She reread it once, twice, and a third time to make sure she read correctly. Dancing with other girls? One girl in particular?

"Jean?" Marge asked. "Are you okay?"

A fire lit in her chest and rolled down into her limbs. Jean ripped the letter in half then tore it to tiny shreds, chucking it onto the floor. She dropped her face into the blanket and barely felt the warmth of her sister's arms through the flame.

The Gift of Gossamer

The rage continued to burn from the letter yesterday. Jean had been loyal to Bob this whole time. She slammed the cash drawer shut, surprising the young couple in front of her. Enjoy your fun while it lasts, she thought.

"Thank you and come see us again," she said with a forced smile. They took their change and hustled out the door.

Bob only wrote that letter because he probably already met someone else and didn't want to get in trouble. The bell jingled announcing another customer. Jean glared at the ring on her finger. He wanted to have his cake and eat it, too.

"Good afternoon, beautiful." Sam smiled with those ridiculous dimples.

The heat coming from her eyes could have melted a glacier.

"Is this the girl?" John wore the same button-up work shirt that Sam did, except the collar of his was neater, not as frayed. While Sam's hair was a sandy color, John's was almost black.

"Sure is," Sam said with a wink.

The doorbells jingled again. Marge stood behind John, mouth agape. Neither man turned to see the new arrival. Sam leaned closer. "What are you doing tonight, Jean?"

Marge flapped her hands frantically. Jean gritted her teeth.

John laughed. "How many times you heard her say no? At least a hundred now. Come on, I'm hungry."

"All I need is one yes. How about we go out tonight?"

Marge's eyes went wide, and she nodded her head up and

down in exaggerated motions. Was this what it was like for Bob? One girl chasing him until he caved? Jean doubted it. Most likely he pursued her—made a plan for conquest and acted it out. Heat singed the tips of her ears. He wanted her to go out with other men...

"Fine."

Sam blinked several times. "Really?"

"Yes."

Marge hopped up and down, clapping her hands. John turned around at the commotion.

"We'll all go," Jean said, nodding at Marge. "We'll meet you at Green Globe at 6:30."

Sam smiled so wide she could see just about every tooth. "I'll see you then." He put both hands in his work pants and whistled as he walked to his usual booth.

Marge stared at John's retreating form. "I can't believe it!" she squealed.

Jean rubbed her neck and looked up at the ceiling. What had she done?

Polka music thumped through the nightclub. The band played with an enthusiasm Jean didn't feel. She drank the last gulp of her Blue Moon and watched Marge bounce on the dance floor with John. At least her sister was having a good time. Sam maneuvered around a couple next to her and handed her a fresh bottle. She had to hand it to him, he'd been respectful and polite, a perfect gentleman. She'd been looking for any reason to end this outing but had yet to find one.

"Wanna dance?" He nodded to the crowded dance floor.

Bob might be dancing with other girls, or rather one girl, at that very moment. "Yes, I do," Jean said. They set their drinks on a table.

Sam's hand felt warm in her own, surprisingly soft for a bricklayer. He led her to an open spot, waited for the beat, then guided her in a lively circle. Marge gave a quick thumbs up before swinging away with John. Sam spun Jean to the left and stepped on her toe. She pretended not to notice and kept up with the rhythm. Then he stepped on her other foot before turning the wrong direction.

"What are you doing?" Jean laughed.

"I'm not very good at this." A faint blush tinted his cheeks.

"Then why do you always ask me to go dancing?"

"I thought you liked it."

Jean looked at the blue eyes searching hers. She sighed. He didn't deserve her anger about Bob. Putting her hand on his arm, she pulled him back over to the table with their drinks.

"Why don't we just talk over here? Tell me about your work." She took a swig of her beer.

He shrugged. "Not much to say. I do mostly bricklaying but other odd jobs whenever I get a chance. I like to help my mom with the bills. And getting to know folks around town."

"You certainly are friendly."

"What made you say yes?"

Jean almost dropped her drink. She couldn't say the words without either howling with rage or bursting into tears. She picked at the label on her bottle trying to think of what to say.

"You don't have to tell me," he said and placed a calming hand over hers to stop her picking. "I'm just glad you're here." He gave a quick squeeze then let go. "Tell me about your brothers and sisters."

The music thumped on as Sam and Jean spent the rest of the evening talking, never broaching the dancefloor again.

Jean turned the dandelion over in her hand. She set it on her dresser next to some Queen Anne's lace. Every day Sam stopped by on his lunch break with a wildflower and a smile for her. She had quite a collection at this point. Even though most of them were dried up and pretty sorry looking, she couldn't manage to get rid of them. They gave some color to her currently gray days.

Marge flopped down on the bed with a thud. She stared up at the ceiling. "Do you think Mom will like him?"

"Does it really matter?" Marge had invited Sam and John over for dinner, much to her dismay. Jean hadn't said anything to her mother about *the letter* and didn't know how she would explain her guest.

"Of course it matters! This man could be my husband."

"Oh. You meant John."

Marge rolled over and smiled, revealing the slight gap between her front teeth. "You know, I really like Sam—"

"Marge!"

"He's nicer to you than Bob is. He...just...thinks about you more, you know? He's very thoughtful. And sweet. And he makes you laugh."

"I already made a promise to someone else." The ring weighed heavy on her finger.

"He doesn't seem very serious about that promise."

Jean looked over at the sister who was often confused as her twin. She had the same hair, same eyes, and the same shaped mouth. Jean knew every inch of that face, including how Marge's left eye twitched the slightest bit if she was hiding something...like it was doing now. "What is it, Marge?"

Marge took a deep breath and pulled a folded envelope out of her pocket. "You were so upset about the other one. I didn't want you to be hurt again."

Jean looked at the proffered letter. "Did you open it?"

"It was already open when I found it in the mailbox."

Uh huh.

Jean snatched the envelope. The familiar handwriting started the flames anew. She hadn't responded to *the letter* and didn't care what was written on this one. Bob made his wishes known, and whether or not he regretted it, his decision had already been made. She grabbed the newest letter and tore it in half, tossing the pieces into the trash can. She couldn't read another entreaty to be with other women.

The doorbell rang downstairs.

Alighting from the bed, Marge yelled, "I'll get it!"

Jean wiped a stray tear from her cheek, straightened her hair, and headed for the stairs. The door stood open, and Marge backed away, a frown pulling down her cheeks.

"John's sick."

The words were lost to Jean when she saw Sam standing on the porch with a half-dozen pink roses. He helped pay the bills for his mother and other siblings. He really shouldn't have wasted good money on flowers that could have been spent on food or clothes.

"Hi, Jean," he said. He handed her three of the roses. "The rest are for your mom. You look beautiful." He pressed a quick kiss on her cheek as he walked in.

"Here," she said, taking the other three roses. "I'll put these in a vase. Mom's busy cooking dinner right now."

Jean pulled the silk flowers out of a vase in the hallway, filled it in the bathroom, and arranged the pink roses. She leaned in and inhaled their subtle, sweet fragrance. "Thank you," she said to Sam who watched her with a contented grin.

"Dinner's ready!" Jean's mother called from the kitchen.

The younger siblings bounded down the stairs and hopped into their seats. Marge waved Sam in. "Mom, this is Sam. He's a new friend, eats lunch at The Waiting Room every day."

Hedya Bendekgey emigrated from Syria at sixteen, managing the weeks-long boat ride over while carrying her first child. Jean's mother had been pregnant fifteen times, given birth to thirteen children, and lived through losing two of the thirteen. Like coal to diamonds, life's pressure turned her into something hard yet beautiful. She worked tirelessly every single day, never missing a detail, and wanting perfection for her home and her children. Her shrewd eyes evaluated the new guest, scanning over Marge and Jean with speculation.

Jean swallowed.

"What is this?" her mother asked, putting her finger in a hole near the seam of Sam's sleeve.

"Mom!" Jean pulled him away and toward an empty chair.

"Thank you for having me over for dinner," he said as he sat. He unfolded the paper napkin and set it in his lap. "This looks delicious." A giant steaming pot of chicken soup and rice sat in the middle of the table.

"Sam is a bricklayer," Marge said. She ladled herself a bowl then passed the spoon to Sam. "He can build just about anything. Isn't that right, Sam?"

Jean twisted her napkin. Why was he in her house? This didn't feel right.

"I do a little bit here and there. Hard work pays off." He smiled at Jean's mother who didn't return it, then passed the rolls. "And I enjoy working on different projects."

"Is that so?" Jean's brother Lou said from across the table. "I got a drug store I'm remodeling. I could use another pair of hands."

"I'd be happy to help."

Jean blanched. She opened her mouth to protest. Her mother gave her a curious stare. Jean closed her mouth.

"Not sure what your rates are—"

"Don't worry about that. I can come by on weekends and do what I can."

Sam would be hanging around her family even more. Even Bob's girl wasn't hanging around his house. For the rest of the meal she ate quietly, watching Sam charm her siblings. At least Mom wasn't falling for it.

"You better catch that last streetcar, Sam," Jean's mother said after they'd sat at the table for over an hour.

"I'd like to stay a bit longer if that's all right." He winked at Jean.

Jean's mother added a scoop of instant grains to her already black coffee. She stirred and stared at him.

"Your soup was delicious," he said. "I loved the rice you put in first. How is it made?"

Great. He found mom's weak spot.

"Boiled butter. That's the trick." Mom leaned back in the chair, her shoulders relaxing.

"You're an excellent cook."

Jean rolled her eyes. Mom had to be seeing through this.

Her mother got up from her chair and returned to the table with a round tin. Popping the lid, she revealed a mound of chocolate chip cookies.

Sam looked inside, probably noting how each cookie had exactly four chocolate chips.

Mom mistook his curiosity for hesitation. "One won't make you fat."

He took two.

Mom beamed.

Marge, Lou, her siblings...and now Mom. Jean had quite enough. She stood. "Why don't we go out on the porch?" Maybe the closer he was to the road the sooner he would leave and quit inveigling her whole family.

They stepped into the twilight and sat on the swing next to the honeysuckle vine. Sam handed her a cookie. Of course he would share. She took it, turning it over in her hand. This whole thing with Sam was going further than she wanted, faster too. He was a nice guy, but this wasn't the right time. Maybe if she'd never...no. She wouldn't go there. She still hadn't made up her mind about Bob yet. Stars glittered above like dewdrops on a spider web. Tangles of silk seemed to be closing in around her, keeping her from reaching her dream.

"You seem upset," Sam said and took a bite of his cookie. "Is it about the letter?"

Jean snapped her head back to him. "What?"

"Marge told me about it."

The cookie turned into sugary sand in her hand. She was going to kill Marge.

"That's a rotten thing to do, putting you in a position like that," he continued.

Jean dumped the cookie remains and dusted her palm.

"I guess it worked out in my favor, though."

"It's time for you to leave." Jean stood.

Sam put his hand on her arm. "I'm sorry. I didn't mean to upset you."

"Then why are you talking about this?" Jean pulled her arm

away. "Why are you even here?"

Sam stood and stepped close to her. "Because you're beautiful and smart and funny and I've been wanting to spend time with you for months."

Bob never talked to her like that. Jean couldn't breathe. She took a step back. The web tightened further, gossamer twisting around her heart.

"I'm sorry. I can't do this." She rushed inside and up the stairs, closing the door to the bedroom behind her. Tears flowed down her cheeks. She couldn't tell if they were from what already happened or what could never be.

Another letter sat in Jean's hands. What if Bob changed his mind about dancing with other girls? Would she have to tell Sam she couldn't see him anymore? She swallowed the knot in her throat. All she'd been thinking about the past several days is what Sam said to her that night on the porch and how kind he'd been since. The letter drifted down into the trash can. Jean met Marge outside.

"Still mad at me?" Marge asked. They walked toward the streetcar stop where they were meeting John and Sam to go to Notes together. Layers of heat danced over the cement.

Jean scowled at her sister and wiped the sweat from around her mouth. She hadn't spoken to her since she found out about Marge's big blabbering mouth.

"Tonight should be fun," Marge went on. "I heard they're having a dance contest. I think I can get John to enter. Maybe you and Sam—"

"I don't think so." She almost laughed at the thought of Sam in a dance contest.

"Ha! Now you're talking to me again." Marge chuckled and tripped, almost falling off the curb. Jean grabbed her arm and pulled her wayward sister back on balance.

"Should have let you fall."

"But then I might get hurt and wouldn't win the dance contest. The prize is a free dinner at Jack's."

Marge chattered the whole way to the stop where Sam and John waited. Jean wore a robin's egg blue dress that accentuated her curves and matched Sam's eyes. She'd been hiding this one in the closet for when Bob came back but knew she made the right choice when she noted Sam's appreciative appraisal. He held a daisy that he promptly tucked behind her ear.

"Hello, beautiful." A kiss on the cheek.

After a quick ride, they arrived.

Notes had previously been a small church, the pews removed for the dance floor, the vestibule now a bar. People on the altar now preached in bouncing measure with their instruments. John held open the heavy oak door. A wave of music mixed with the heat of dancing tumbled onto the street. Couples crowded the dance floor. Marge launched into the foray, but Jean held back. She didn't care for the noise of the clubs anymore. All she really wanted to do was talk to Sam.

"Do you mind if we stay out here?" She motioned toward a patio with candlelit tables overlooking the Ohio River. Steel mills lined the banks on the opposite side, looking like abandoned cities with darkened towers next to the hopping club, a mix of

275

excitement tinged with darkness.

Sam guided her past the tables and over to the railing where they had a clear view of the calm water. He kept his hand on the small of her back.

"You see that part of the riverbank down there that stretches out into the water?" he asked after a time.

Jean nodded.

"When we were younger, my sister and I were mad at our mom, for what I can't remember now, but we decided to make a raft like Huck Finn. You know, set off down the river for freedom."

Jean laughed. Sounded like something her and Marge would do.

"So we stuffed our beds full of clothes from the closet, grabbed a bunch of rope from the shed, and took off. It's quite a walk from our house to here, and Sis whined the whole way. She fell in a blackberry bush at one point and got scratched up and was absolutely miserable. Couldn't shut her up. I was already regretting bringing her along. Anyway, we finally got here and started collecting wood—I mean scrawny little sticks and half-rotted logs, real quality building materials. I tied the ends together with the rope and realized we didn't bring a knife to cut it. So we both screamed at each other, making all kinds of racket. We didn't hear anyone coming until Mom was about ten feet away. Boy, she was madder than a hornet's nest. I swore I actually saw the smoke coming from her ears. Me and Sis panicked and tossed our 'raft' in the water and tried to hop on. Well of course the thing fell apart, and we were just climbing on top of a pile of sticks in the shallows."

"Why didn't you just swim?"

"I never said we were the brightest kids. Mom came up to us—and to this day I don't know how she had the strength—but somehow she lifted both of us out of the water. She held one of us in each hand and dragged our butts back home. And I thought Sis whined on the way there. That was nothing compared to the ruckus she made going home. We got whipped for running away, getting all wet, and for wrinkling the clothes from the closet."

Jean couldn't stop laughing. A redhead at a nearby table gave her a strange look, but she didn't care.

"Mom was on to us immediately. Said the neighbors all heard Sis whining the whole way and told her where we went. We had to iron all the clothes we wrinkled. Sis kept fussing saying her hands hurt from where the blackberry bush scratched her, so I ended up doing it all."

"That was nice of you."

"What can I say? I'm a nice guy."

Jean leaned closer to Sam. He really was a nice guy—always bringing her flowers, even some for her mom, helping Lou with the pharmacy. And of course assisting his mother with the bills. No wonder he had so many friends. Who wouldn't like someone as kind and giving as him? Jean liked him, liked him more than she let herself think before.

Sam seemed to pick up on Jean's thoughts and pulled her against him. She rested her hands on his arms. They seemed to fit there.

"I'm glad you finally said yes."

"Me too."

He pressed his lips to hers in a soft kiss, lingering for a moment. It felt so right, so natural, like breathing. They stayed there the rest of the evening, looking at the stars and exchanging sweet kisses while the music danced in the air around them.

Jean twisted the ring on her finger and threw yet another letter from Bob in the trash. She'd have to make a decision soon. She'd been going on dates with Sam for almost two months now and knew it wasn't fair to pretend this was going somewhere if it really wasn't. But she had made a promise to Bob and already laid out her future. She couldn't change it now, could she?

She headed into the kitchen and pulled out the bag of potatoes. Her parents had left town for the weekend, and she and Marge were supposed to take care of the cooking. Where was Marge anyway? She was supposed to be home fifteen minutes ago. The potatoes thudded into the pot with a little more force than necessary. Jean chopped the rosemary and tossed it in with the spuds. The screen door whacked closed.

"You were supposed to be here fifteen minutes ago."

"Sorry," Sam said. "Didn't know we had an appointment."

Jean turned with a smile. "What are you doing here?"

"Me and Lou just finished up for the day and he invited me over for dinner."

"He's using my homemade meals as payment?" she said, snorting.

Sam sniffed the air and curled his arms around her waist. "That's like getting paid overtime." He pressed a kiss to her cheek.

"Want some help?"

She tossed more rosemary into the pot and reached for the onions. "I'm sure you're tired from working all day. Aren't you sick of busting your behind every Saturday?"

He grinned. "Gives me an extra chance to see you." He gave her another kiss then washed his hands in the sink. Opening the icebox, he peered inside. "How about I get started on this chicken?"

The two talked and prepared the food, then sat together at the table while everyone ate. Marge burst through the door halfway through the meal sputtering something about missing the streetcar. Jean didn't really mind. She liked her cooking partner. But that didn't mean Marge was totally off the hook.

"You clean up. We're going out on the porch." Jean grabbed two beers and smiled when Sam opened the door for her.

They snuggled together on the swing, swaying back and forth while not saying much at all. It was peaceful. It was perfect. They soon started telling each other stories from their childhood, laughing while the hours passed and sneaking in a few kisses. A frog croaked nearby. Jean looked at her watch. It was well past a respectable hour in which to have a male visitor, especially one that wasn't her fiancé. Lucky for her it didn't matter this weekend. She pulled Sam in for a long kiss.

He shifted back. "Jeanie, I've been thinking. It's about your engagement. I want...I mean...you mean a lot to me and...I am asking you to—"

Headlights lit up the street as a very familiar '48 Chevy Fleetline came closer. "My parents!" Jean shouted. She bolted off the swing. "You have to go. Now!"

Scrambling from the swing, Sam hopped over the porch railing and made his way through the bushes to the back of the house. What the heck were her parents doing coming back at 2 AM? It didn't matter. She couldn't get caught out. The car turned down the driveway, lighting up the front door. They'd see her going inside. She needed to get to her room fast. She took one look at the trellis and knew what she had to do.

Throwing the beer bottles along the side of the house, she put her foot in the honeysuckle vines and hefted herself up.

The car doors shut.

Jean almost lost her balance at the sound. She flattened herself halfway up the trellis as her parents approached the porch.

Don't look over. Don't look over.

The front door banged closed.

Jean hurled herself up the rest of the way and tiptoed across the roof to her window. She squeezed inside. Almost there. She padded across the room to the bed and lifted the blankets.

Footsteps thudded on the stairs.

Marge stirred awake and her eyes widened in panic. "Ahhh—"

Jean slapped a hand over her sister's mouth. "Shhhh! It's me."

The footsteps stopped outside the door. The knob turned.

Jean leaped into bed and pulled the covers up. She closed her eyes and forced herself to breathe rhythmically, hoping the outline of her shoes under the sheets wouldn't give her away.

The door closed and Jean released a long breath.

"What's going on?"

"Nothing. Go back to sleep."

Jean took off her clothes and slipped into a nightgown. Her eyelids shuttered while a distant thought floated through. *What was he going to say?*

Three stacks of bills sat on the counter next to The Waiting Room register. Jean had counted them four times and gotten different numbers every time. She sighed. Something was off about today, and she couldn't quite put her finger on it. She picked up the nearest stack and tried again. *20, 40, 60, what was Sam going to say about the engagement?*

She tossed down the money. Again. They'd only been going on dates for a short while. He had no right to tell her what to do. He was the one who pushed into her life, a life she already had planned out. Nevermind that Bob screwed it all up. Jean slammed the register drawer closed, and turned her back to it, crossing her arms over her chest. Sam had been like a garden spider, throwing out strand after strand of silk for months, slowly closing in on her, until she couldn't move. This was *her* life. She refused to be trapped by anyone.

A knock sounded on the glass door.

"We're closed!" Jean yelled without turning around.

Another knock.

She flipped around to see Sam standing there with those damn blue eyes again. She needed to know what he was going to say.

The door unlocked with a click and he pushed it open, right into her space. "What were you saying?" she demanded.

Sam's eyebrows shot up. "What are you talking about, Jeanie?"

"Don't you call me that. About my engagement. What were you saying?"

Sam rubbed the back of his neck. "Well...I...um...want you to break it."

"That's my decision!"

"I know. But I want you to be with me."

"You've made that very clear. You bring me flowers and...and..." the anger stole the words from her. He just pushed, pushed, pushed into her life. "You do all these things all the time. Like my brother. Why do you spend every weekend helping him? Why?"

"Because I love you."

Jean gasped.

He loved her. Of course he did. He was kind and giving and funny and sweet...everything she could ever want. Everything she did want. She wanted to make her own life. Now she would.

"There's something I need to do. Meet me at my house at seven."

The yellow house sat on a small lot on "the island," a piece of land by Wheeling, West Virginia. Jean knocked three times and remembered the dinners she had over here and how welcoming

Bob's mother had been. She always gushed over Jean, calling her a second daughter.

Alpha opened the door, and a huge smile stretched across her face. "I haven't seen you in so long." She gripped Jean in a tight hug. "I've been meaning to invite you over for dinner. It's just been so busy. I completely forgot. They put me in charge of the church raffle and Darren came down with colitis and—"

"Alpha." Jean extricated herself from the woman's grip.

"But you look so nice. That chocolate color really compliments your eyes. Did I ever tell you my grandmother made the best chocolates? She put walnuts in them and they just melted in your mouth and—"

"Alpha. I can't stay. I have something I need to give you."

"Oh?"

Jean took a deep breath. She pulled the ring off her finger and handed it to Bob's mother. "Tell Bob good luck with that girl he's been seeing."

For once Alpha was speechless.

"Thank you for always being kind to me." And with that Jean turned and left her now ex future mother-in-law.

Streaks of vibrant orange lit up the evening sky. Jean breathed in the sweet honeysuckle and massaged the bare skin on her ring finger. On her hand, a white strip stood out where the band once hugged her skin. She'd gotten used to the ring and its security in such a short time, not thinking about what her heart really wanted.

And he was walking toward her with a violet in his hand. She couldn't keep the smile off her face or the flutter in her heart to slow down.

"Hey, Jeanie." Sam tucked the violet behind her ear then stood back further than usual. "What's going on?"

Jean took the flower from behind her ear, fingering the petals. "You always have so much to give. Now I have something to give you."

Jean held up her left hand and wiggled her empty ring finger.

Sam gasped and grabbed Jean. "Let's go tell Mom," Jean said, taking Sam and her future in her hands.

He lifted her above him and spun in a circle. Jean laughed and held him close when she was back on her feet.

Gossamer twisted around them, cocooning Jean and Sam together forever.

Get an update on Jean and Sam and see pictures at www.orangeblossombooks.com

Book Club Discussion Questions

1. How does the uniqueness of the Antarctica setting impact the development of Michelle and Brandon's relationship? (*A Rose, Frozen in Time*)

2. Do you think Sister Baptiste went to Michael and Deborah's wedding? Why or why not? (*Love in Marabella*)

3. Would Chelsea and Brandon have gotten together if he hadn't done the not-friends-anymore tactic? Why or why not? (*A Heart Guarded*)

4. How does an artichoke represent (or not represent) Paige and Matt as a couple? (*Cute Hat Boy and the Weird Girl*)

5. When did it seem like Eddie fully committed to Bob? (*Eddie and Me*)

6. Why do you think Melody wasn't discouraged when she found out she was part of Myke's "harem?" (*All I Did Was Open the Door*)

7. Who seemed to change the most, Tim or Arielle, from the first date to the second? Why? (*Out of the Park*)

8. How did Greg show KJ he was a good match for her? (*Reacquainting*)

9. When have you had previous unknown encounters with people the way Cheryl and Ken had? (*In the Cards*)

10. Which meal do you think had a bigger impact on Valerie and Justin's relationship, the spaghetti or the chili? (*Never Feed Spaghetti To a Stray*)

11. Did Fern's hairdresser impact any decisions she made about dating? (*Die Laughing*)

12. How did Anthony go from someone who annoyed Kerry to a good friend? (*City Nights*)

13. What seemed to be the turning point for Louise, when she softened towards Bud? (*Amazing Grace*)

14. What do you think Julianna expected for herself

and her life when she moved to the U.S.? (*Two Hungarian Doves*)

15. What was the biggest factor for Jean not reading Bob's letters: her anger at his betrayal or avoiding him while her feelings for Sam grew? (*The Gift of Gossamer*)

16. Which element seemed to play the most prominent role in most of the stories: timing, opportunity, open-mindedness, or the willingness to take risks?

17. What story seemed to have the biggest odds against the couple getting together?

18. Which person seemed to be the most surprised when they found their love?

19. Do you believe any of the couples had "love at first sight?" If so, which ones?

20. Which story was similar to a love story in your life (yours, your parents, relatives...)?

Meet the Authors

Michelle Tweed
A Rose, Frozen in Time

Michelle Tweed enjoys writing children's adventure books, historical fiction and non-fiction, and personal development. She is currently working on a book about her own adventures.

Michelle lives in beautiful Minnesota Lakes Country, with her husband, two kids, and two Australian Shepherds. When she's not having fun with her family, or working her Lake Home business, you can probably find her walking a plowed field collecting stone artifacts, out enjoying nature, or mentoring women through her blog, www.learning2letgo.com. You can see her latest projects at www.MichelleTweed.com.

Be sure to check out Michelle's update at Orange Blossom Publishing to see how the rose has continued to hold special and unexpected meaning in her life.

Racquel Henry
Love in Marabella

Racquel Henry is a Trinidadian writer and editor with an MFA from Fairleigh Dickinson University. She is also a part-time English Professor and owns the writing center, Writer's Atelier, in Winter Park, FL. In 2010 Racquel co-founded Black Fox Literary Magazine where she still serves as an editor. She is also a board member for The Jack Kerouac Project, an Orlando-based writing residency. Her fiction, poetry, and nonfiction have appeared in places like Lotus-Eater Magazine, Moko Caribbean Arts & Letters, Thrill of the Hunt: Welcome to Whitebridge, Reaching Beyond the Saguaros: A Collaborative Prosimetric Travelogue (Serving House Books, 2017), We Can't Help It If We're From Florida (Burrow Press, 2017), and The Writer's Atelier Little Book of Writing Affirmations (Writer's Atelier, 2018), among others. She loves Instagram, find her: @RacquelHenry or @WritersAtelier. You can also visit www.racquelhenry.com.

Chelsea Fuchs
A Heart Guarded

Chelsea Fuchs is an avid reader of sweet romances and management books and writes strong female leads in nontraditional roles. Her background as a chemical engineer and cowgirl heavily influence her characters and stories. After spending nearly a decade in the engineering field writing and reviewing government documents, she changed careers to be a stay at home mom with her two energetic children. When she's not busy keeping her littles from taking over the world or explaining chemical reactions one mess at a time, she's writing women's fiction and planning for the day that she and her husband buy a cattle ranch and ride off into the sunset. Chelsea lives in New Mexico with her (almost) high school sweetheart, their son and daughter, a dog, four chickens, a rooster, and a sucker fish that just won't die.

Paige Lavoie
Cute Hat Boy and the Weird Girl

Paige Lavoie is a vintage-loving YA Author from Orlando FL. She writes Coming of Age stories about geek girls, outsiders, and monsters! Paige loves telling stories about characters who find strength in themselves and create long-lasting friendships along the way. When she's not writing, Paige makes motivational pep talk videos for local writing community Writer's Atelier and streams creating-writing and video games on her twitch channel. She can often be spotted strolling arm-in-arm with her husband hunting for antiques to furnish their 1950s home. She blogs about daily life, inspiration, and writing on www.paigelavoie.com and her books can be found on Amazon. Visit www.paigelavoie.wordpress.com.

Robert Bellam
Eddie and Me

Author Robert Bellam has had seven submissions published out of ten in the digital, multimedia market within the past year. He is working on the third revision of his current manuscript, *A Man of Many Pleasures*, soon to be published. During the past twelve years he has been the facilitator of a writers' critique group in Clermont, Florida.

Prior to becoming a fiction writer, Bob served as an Administrator for the Prince George's County Maryland Health Department's disease control programs. Also, as a Grant Writer and facilitator for the distribution of Federal Funding for Suburban Maryland.

Melody Groves
All I Did Was Open the Door

Full-time freelance writer Melody Groves lives a wild and wooly life. Travelling the world, she meets amazing people while researching locales and history. Melody spent her "growing up" years on Guam and in the Philippines, where she encountered "friendly" headhunters, ran into alligator-sized iguanas, and was harassed by a belligerent band of monkeys. However, the American West captured her heart.

A deep love of anything cowboy and Old West creates a fertile playground for her imagination. In ten years with the New Mexico Gunfighters, she learned what it feels like going toe-to-

toe with shotgun-wielding sheriffs and quick-draw outlaws. "The bullets may be blanks, but the adrenaline is real." Playing both "good guy" and "bad guy" gives her a firsthand feel for what her western fiction characters experience.

Bull riding school gave her a deep understanding and appreciation for the sport of rodeo. It led to her creating the first rodeo book of its kind. She learned being thrown high and coming down hard is tough, bruising but exhilarating.

She is author of the award-winning *Colton Brothers Saga* series of 1860s southern New Mexico/Arizona and also pens the *She Was Sheriff* series of 1872 northern California. In addition, several non-fiction books, frequent contributions for *True West, Enchantment, New Mexico* (et. al) magazines and in-depth research fills her awards shelf with plaques and trophies.

When not writing, she teaches writing courses, is in demand as a public speaker and plays rhythm guitar with the Jammy Time Band.

Timothy Haughee
Out of the Park

Tim Haughee is an in-house attorney for Darden Restaurants, Inc., where he spends much of his writing efforts on legal briefs. Tim was born, raised, and currently lives in Orlando, Florida with his more-talented wife, Arielle, and his two young boys, Luke and Caleb.

Greg Hill
Reacquainting

Greg Hill is an adjunct professor in English, a math tutor, a voice over talent and a poet. He has a creative writing MALS degree from Dartmouth College and an MFA in Writing from Vermont College of Fine Arts. His work has appeared in *Atlas and Alice, Queen Mob's Teahouse, Life and Legends, Whiskey Island* and elsewhere. In his free time he cultivates his interests in quantum physics, musical cryptography and toki pona. He and his wife KJ and their three daughters live in West Hartford, CT. Website: www.gregjhill.com.

Cheryl Dougherty
In the Cards

Cheryl Dougherty is a retired educator who lives in New Smyrna Beach, FL with her husband, Ken. A graduate of the University of Connecticut, Cheryl has recently begun work on a series of children's books. *In the Cards* is her first published work.

Valerie Willis
Never Feed Spaghetti to a Stray

Valerie Willis, a sixth generation Floridian, launched her first book, *Cedric the Demonic Knight*, at the start of 2012 on Amazon.com. Since then, she has continued to add to *The Cedric Series,* a high-rated Paranormal Fantasy Romance Series featuring an anti-hero who finds himself dragged away from his revenge on his maker by both love and the onset of a larger threat. She pulls in a melting pot of mythology, folklores, history and more into her work with a remarkable amount of foreshadowing that makes reading her books a second time exciting. *Rebirth* is the first book in her Teen Urban Fantasy, the *Tattooed Angels Trilogy* where the main character struggles with social issues with the complications of turning immortal. And if fantasy isn't your cup of tea, head over to her blog for some "Val, Tell me a Story" posts featuring true, hilarious, and sometimes bizarre, life events from old to recent. Visit www.willisauthor.com.

Fern Goodman
Die Laughing

Fern Goodman is an award-winning author and poet. A Michigan girl in a Florida world, her background in travel and event planning has been replaced with life coaching and authoring.

Her first book was a collaboration with her sister, of musings about dogs, mirroring her sisters' original photography; *Captured...the look of the dog*. Other short stories of hers appear in various anthologies: *Lost Dreams, Important Firsts, What a Character, Demonic Household, Where does your Muse live?* and *Work of Hearts Magazine*. Fern's specialty is reality humor, which she demonstrates on YouTube, Fern at the Stardust Lounge. Although her latest non-fiction Kindle short read, *Shooting UP Hope*, is not a humorous subject, Fern finds a way to soften the mood of tragic events.

Kerry Evelyn
City Nights

Kerry Evelyn has always been fascinated by people and the events in their lives that drive them to do what they do. A native of the Massachusetts SouthCoast, she changed her latitude in 2002 to teach in Florida and is now a crazy blessed wife and homeschooling mom near the Happiest Place on Earth. She is the author of the *Crane's Cove* series, an inspirational romance set in picturesque Coastal Maine featuring stories of people hurting on the inside and their journeys from broken to happily ever after. Kerry is a member of several local and national writing organizations, a mentor to aspiring authors, and workshop presenter. She loves God, books of all kinds, traveling, taking selfies, sweet drinks, and escaping into her imagination where every child is happy and healthy, every house has a library, and her hubby wears coattails and a top hat 24/7. Visit www.kerryevelyn.com.

John Hope
Amazing Grace

Currently at home in Central Florida, John Hope loves spending time with this family and friends. Whether he's traveling thousands of miles in a car or playing board games on the living room floor, he loves the company and conversations and laughs with the ones he loves. He often pulls from these times with his family and loved ones to create wonderfully tender moments and hilariously vivid characters in his writing.

Shortly after marrying the love of his life, John was blessed with the birth of his daughter and son. Reading night after night to his kids, he revived his writing by making up stories for his kids. This lead to a number of published books that came directly from these stories: *The Band Aid, Frozen Floppies*, and *Pankyland*. He still works as a software engineer, a career he enjoys at times, but his heart remains in his writing. Visit www.johnhopewriting.com.

Jasmine Tritten
Two Hungarian Doves

Jasmine Tritten is an artist, writer and world traveler born in Denmark. She loves to write and has been journaling since childhood. Jasmine has written numerous short stories during the last five years that have been published in various journals and anthologies.

Her memoir, *The Journey of an Adventuresome Dane,* was published in 2015 and won an award. She wrote and illustrated her latest book, *Kato's Grand Adventure,* a children's story, which was published in July 2018. The short story, *Two Hungarian Doves,* was inspired after a trip to Hungary visiting relatives of her spouse. You can find her books on Amazon.

Jasmine resides in enchanting Corrales, New Mexico with her husband and five cats.

Arielle Haughee
The Gift of Gossamer

Previously an elementary teacher, Arielle Haughee (Hoy) is a multi-genre author living in the Orlando area. She has a serious reading addiction, fantasy romance her absolute favorite, and loves nothing more than good conversation paired with a good wine. She is surrounded by males at home—a husband, two sons, and an energetic dog—and tries to integrate as much purple and flowers in the house as possible.

Arielle is the owner of Orange Blossom Publishing and the author of children's picture books *Grumbler* and *Joyride* (2019). She also writes short fiction for a number of anthologies and publications. She's won three Royal Palm Literary Awards including First Place Published Flash Fiction for "Flight of a New Dawn" in 2018. She is currently finishing up work on *The Light Wielder*, a fantasy romance novel, scheduled for release in 2020. Visit www.ariellehaughee.com.

A Sneak Peek. . .

...at the next installment of How I Met My Other:

Furry Friends!

Our next volume in the anthology series will feature fun stories of how people became matched up with their beloved pets. Coming February 1, 2020!

Connect with Us

Connect with Orange Blossom Publishing

Stay up to date with new releases and upcoming projects by signing up for our newsletter at www.orangeblossombooks.com.

Connect with us on Facebook and Instagram, @orange_blossom_books.

How Did We Do?

Want to see more Anthologies like this one?
Had a favorite story you want to comment on?
Want to share your reading experience?
The best gift you can give an author is a review.

If you enjoyed the book, we'd love for you to leave us a review on Amazon or Goodreads.